RAPE OF AMERICA

EDMOND ROBERTSON

authorHOUSE®

AuthorHouse™
1663 Liberty Drive, Suite 200
Bloomington, IN 47403
www.authorhouse.com
Phone: 1-800-839-8640

First published by AuthorHouse   5/24/2007

ISBN: 978-1-4343-1694-3 (sc)

Printed in the United States of America
Bloomington, Indiana

This book is printed on acid-free paper.

DEDICATION!

THIS BOOK IS DEDICATED TO all the Real Americans who have made the ultimate sacrifice from 1776 until today. It is hoped their sacrifices will not be betrayed by our elected officials. America must remain a nation of people dedicated to the original concept and deadly sacrifices of America's founders. Our leaders must not be allowed to continue betraying America whatever the cost! To hand the nation over to hordes of foreign illegal invaders is traitorous to the memory of those who died protecting America's traditions and integrity and will spell certain doom for America! There are many who say and believe the Iraq travesty was a deliberate plan to make illegal immigration less noticeable until the hordes of ignorant invaders had secured the country. Many of our top leaders once respected are now displaying their true colors and they are not Red, White or Blue! Insipid and insidious plans are under way by a consortium of traitors at this moment to include the capitulation of American sovereignty to the embodiment of a North American Union composed of Mexico, Canada, and the United States. This is typical of a crowd who call themselves the "Elite" or superior beings. The current thrust of efforts is to plunge the knife of deceit into backs of Americans and devise means and ways to bypass the United States Senate and Congress by any subterfuge. It is regrettable that people who are trusted by American citizens are in reality turncoats that equal Benedict Arnold. If these traitors are not stopped in their tracks America will cease to be a nation of individuals with liberty, justice and opportunity for all, but prisoners of treason, greed and corruption on a scale never before witnessed. America would have no borders, no flag, no unity of purpose, no pride of being an American with a rich heritage of patriotic founders that sacrificed all to provide freedom and justice for their progeny. America will, if these traitors succeed with this dastardly plan, be destroyed forever, placing and casting the failure of America directly in the laps of the majority of our rotten politicians who ignored all the signs and did not censor and control with impeachment and removal from office, the low down executive and legal branches of government who stole America while trusting Americans slept in confidence of the integrity of elected officials.

The Senate and Congress are the two most powerful governmental bodies on earth and through cooperation and an honest desire to work for the historical values of America, can control our borders and the low down rotten crooks attempting to destroy the United States of America. The court of last resort will be the judgement of disgusted American citizens who will resolve and prevent the destruction of America by direct intervention if necessary.

Alexander Solzhenitsyn said:

"A state of war only serves as an excuse for domestic tyranny"!

Destruction of America by unfettered unlimited Illegal Immigration permitted, condoned and approved by G. Bush and low down Senate amnesty proponents is a deadly form of tyranny and they know it but don't care.

Apparently G. Bush thinks he is pulling a fast one through his obvious promotion of flooding America with Mexicans to destroy our nation, thus continuing the efforts of the "Elite" to imprison humanity under a One World Government! If this is denied as a lie, let's hear it why Mr. Bush has been pro-illegal immigration from his very first day as governor of Texas! The arrogance of such behavior is reminiscent of the Nazi plans for ruling the human race as the "Superior" or "Elite" authority. How can people trust a Chief Executive when he was reportedly heard saying "Stop reminding me about the Constitution, it's only a Goddamned piece of paper".

PROLOGUE

PRESIDENT JOHN ADAMS SAID: "DEMOCRACY never lasts long. It soon wastes, exhausts and murders itself. There was never a democracy that did not commit suicide!" April 15, 1814

> A Republic must either preserve its virtue or lose its Liberty!
>
> *John Witherspoon*

THE ONE AND ONLY PURPOSE of this book is to attempt to alert the people of America to the undeniable fact that their country is being stolen from them through traitorous political betrayal from the very top of the political hierarchy to the bottom while they sleep, and hopefully arouse their indignation and patriotism to the point of rising up and cleansing the nation's rotten political structure! The length of the text has been limited to only the information pertinent to providing you, the reader, with a description of the disastrous and evil forces at work which are destroying America - not from the outside - but from within! Identical to Ancient Rome!

America's 230 years of freedom and tradition has now been compromised by politicians to the very edge of the point of no return and if allowed to continue any farther will result in a total collapse of The United States of America. While you were sleeping, greed, subservience to big business racketeers, One World Traitors and indifference by those elected to stand in for us has taken over and sentenced America to death by default if allowed to continue. It is a known fact that most politicians do and will become Liars and Thieves given enough time in office. A moment's reflection will bring to bear the sobering thought that the primary thrust of a politician's actions is concerned with, and driven by, the desire to be re-elected **above all else!** Therefore, to pursue this desire for "the good life" requires the willingness of many to exaggerate, or promise (some call it lying) as to the great guy he (she) is and the wonderful life you will have under his (her) guidance.

At this juncture it becomes obvious he (she) cannot serve two masters – so what shall it be – spend many thousands of taxpayer's dollars praising himself (herself) to influence the voters and get re-elected, or work for America and his (her) constituents?

All one has to do is look at the pitiful and tragic state of America and the answer is clear. The United States of America comes in a distant second place. Don't be misled by appearances – as we all know appearances can be deceiving – you may hear loud denials – "America is going strong", "the economy is great", and other platitudes to lull you into going back to sleep.

The sad truth is our political establishment has, with their total commitment to Political Correctness (a synonym for no guts) allowed the uncontrolled invasion of America to place the nation on the certain path to destruction – there is no denying this truth no matter how many lies and denials may be espoused from guilty lowdown traitorous politicians from all over America!

The unconcern for America's welfare is pathetically apparent and disgraceful as one sees each and every day on television and newspaper reports. Not a day goes by without childlike juvenile confrontations and disgusting personal partisan behavior between the Republicans and Democrats while the nation sinks into eternal oblivion morally and physically!

As you continue you will realize the extent of abandonment of sworn oaths by the majority of our politicians, with the result being the United States of America and all her Real American citizens have been placed in grave danger of extinction!

It is apparent our nation will not survive under the present gangs of so-called leaders from top to bottom in the political structure now handing over the nation to barbarians and destroying the United States of America.

If America is to survive, it's now or never – the Real Americans must wake up and become proactive in demanding - not asking – our so-called leaders to shape up – stand up for America - or else!

Exception Note: We have many representatives who are Real Americans and stand publicly for America and vote against the betrayal of historical American ideals, traditions, and integrity by fellow politicians. America is in their debt!

Unfortunately, they are in a minority to the majority who are hypocrites and traitors to their sworn oaths to protect America.

It is hoped these loyal Real American representatives of the people of the United States will band together to condemn the traitors among them and inform American citizens as to their identity in order for voters to boot them out! Otherwise, the definite possibility of conflict and war in the streets of America exists as Real Americans are forced by cowardly political traitors to reclaim their country!

Rape of America

George Washington said, "Government is not reason, it is not eloquence. It is force. Like fire it is a dangerous servant and a fearful master! Never for a moment should it be left to irresponsible action!"

Is it coincidence or fate that our government has made this quote come true? Many of our political leaders elected to be servants of the people have turned into uncontrolled fearful masters of deceit! This abandonment of sworn oaths is a daily occurrence and totally responsible for America becoming a society of second, third and fourth rate human beings. A nation needs proper direction and guidance, positive morality, opportunity and exemplary examples by leaders chosen to lead them as a successful society!

Now, sadly, many of our leaders have, over the past five decades stepped away from this responsibility in favor of self gratification, pursuing political repayments, internal external party squabbling and placed America in the most precarious position ever faced by a nation.

Patrick Henry said "I know not what path others may take, but as for me, give me liberty or give me death"

In today's insane Politically Correct, and unpatriotic attitude, a statement of this magnitude of conviction would be greeted with derision by today's "modern" gutless politicians of America. It is sickening to realize that America was born from Revolution but is now in the process of committing suicide from apathy and stupidity, perpetuated by many immoral, and corrupt trusted leaders who have weaved this web of deceit into the lives of gullible citizens who mistakenly believe in the integrity of any and all elected officials most of whom only know how to spell "truth", not practice it!

The majority of our elected representatives, for the past fifty plus years, have abandoned the convictions of our great founders of America and chosen instead to plan :

1. For continuing their tenure in office.
2. For their great financial future at taxpayer expense!
3. To spend and waste billions of unauthorized dollars in mostly worthless projects that will enhance their image and re-election.

This makes it virtually impossible to place individual blame on the wasting of billions in taxpayer's money each year. Thus it becomes obvious as to why America is sliding into oblivion: The needs of America and her real citizens come in as a fourth place loser thanks to the combined traitorous policies of politicians all over America conspiring with big business racketeers and foreign governments to dip their hands in the greed barrel.

There is no nation on this earth more corrupt than the United States of America!

In actuality you are a prisoner of the political community - the all powerful wardens and directors of your life parading before your eyes as your loyal representative while stabbing you and your family's future in the back! Never mind the squandering of the levies and blood monies extracted from you! This is none of your business – you are stupid they are geniuses -you are the sheep they are the shepherds! As a dumb Mr. "Ordinary Citizen" you must not question the wisdom and intentions of those who have been elected by you – the people! You must not question how and why most candidates spend millions of dollars to get elected to a job supposedly representing the people, which could not be repaid in two lifetimes even on their excessive salary. Where does this money come from? Corporate entities do not contribute millions for nothing! While campaigning you are the most important and influential person in their lives and they will promise you the moon to get elected. After election you are no more than an irritating bothersome low life state constituent. "Just keep your nose to the grindstone and pay those taxes in order for them to keep living the good life in Washington and State Capitols". Most politicians in general are liars and thieves! Some few are "good guys", and looking out for Real Americans – but they are in the minority! The general opinion is that most are Political Correctness hacks with nothing to contribute to America's survival- just sucking up the unlimited perks and charging it to the taxpayer!

Does this elicit a certain suspicion as to the future activities of these people elected by you to provide improved quality of life for you and your family, prepare for our national defense, better education, protect our borders, control runaway population, regulate immigration which is destroying America, and last but not least; have the guts to stand up for America -not crawl under the table and apologize when criticized by foreigners and the ACLU. Sadly there seems to be a national contagious brain infection peculiar to most of today's politicians which is destroying America's traditions and future as a nation! Taxpayers' money is wasted on under the table deals, personal expenses that are outrageous, totally useless projects to repay contributions, and living the good life in Washington and State Capitols.

In order to pacify you, the "little insignificant voter", from time to time you get the standard line of crapola from your so-called representatives, espousing on how they have "worked for you". In reality, this is a standard BS statement that is used by all politicians to lull constituents into a complacency mode while the various treasuries are being raided and the nation's real problems are ignored.

The following information should convince you that in reality, in the name of greed, jealously, ignorance, cowardice and indifference, America is being betrayed and sold down the river by many of our lying uncaring Politically Correct politicians. So as to be perfectly clear in defining "traitor", here is the Merriam-Webster dictionary description which will be the interpretation used in this text:

One who betrays another's trust or is false to an obligation or duty!

Americans trust our elected representatives to shape and direct America in a path that always includes respect for the Constitution of the United States of America, the sacrifices and truths it represents, and the integration of measures to assure the continuing prosperity and security of America and her legal citizens. The sad predicament of the United States of America is due specifically to the total failure of politicians to ensure that the security and welfare of the United States is not breached and to provide for the internal needs of America – not cowering behind Political Correctness in a useless and mistaken attempt to appease those who will destroy the United States either by fire or destructive ignorant overpopulation. If our politicians really cared about the nation or REAL AMERICANS, they would, themselves, as loyal Americans, declare and pass a minimum five year enforced immigration moratorium, deport all illegal invaders without trials and forget the tripe and crap about "I've got rights." They have no rights – they are foreign criminals – period! America is being hoisted on it's own petard by the slovenly disgusting "chicken" behavior of our so-called leaders!

A large percentage of our so-called leaders in Washington and their "buddies" in state governments spend so much time on personal projects, absenteeism, bowing to influence of powerful big business lobbyists and scheming how to screw their constituents out of more money, that no time and money is left for planning for the controlled growth and security of America! Check the attendance and voting record of a large percentage of your so-called representatives - you will be disgusted!

According to official sources there will be three hundred million human beings in America sometime in October, 2006. That's right - 300 Million! Hispanics have five (5) times the birth rate of responsible Real Americans. This is the reason there are millions wanting to invade America and is due primarily to ignorance which breeds complete disregard for the future welfare of their mostly illegitimate offspring or their nation. This fact is supported by the millions of Illegal Immigrant Criminals breezing into America thanks to George Bush ignoring the danger attached to unlimited, uncontrolled immigration and the cowardly politicians in Washington, Arizona, Texas and

California who are aiding and abetting criminals! There are millions of Real Americans unemployed, their families barely surviving on food stamps and handouts, (McDonald wages) no insurance to help with medical problems, children living in extreme poverty with no chance of ever escaping the trap created by most of these same uncaring, arrogant, gutless people, federal and state, running and ruining America who could rescue these unfortunate souls instead of spending billions for supporting ILLEGAL CRIMINALS!

Consider these magnificent statements of our forefathers included in the Declaration of Independence:

"We hold these truths to be self-evident, that all men are created equal, that they are endowed by their Creator with certain unalienable Rights, that among these are Life, Liberty and the pursuit of Happiness. --That to secure these rights, Governments are instituted among Men, deriving their just powers from the consent of the governed, --That whenever any Form of Government becomes destructive of these ends, it is the Right of the People to alter or to abolish it, and to institute new Government, laying its foundation on such principles and organizing its powers in such form, as to them shall seem most likely to effect their Safety and Happiness. Prudence, indeed, will dictate that Governments long established should not be changed for light and transient causes; and accordingly all experience hath shewn, that mankind are more disposed to suffer, while evils are sufferable, than to right themselves by abolishing the forms to which they are accustomed. But when a long train of abuses and usurpations, pursuing invariably the same Object evinces a design to reduce them under absolute Despotism, it is their right, it is their duty, to throw off such Government, and to provide new Guards for their future security. — Such has been the patient sufferance of these Colonies; and ......"

Today, America is faced with a decaying decadent political system that has systematically abandoned and destroyed the ideals and declarations of our nation's founders.

Liberty and the pursuit of happiness has been reduced to only a catch phrase and a unobtainable dream for the average REAL

AMERICAN struggling to escape the treacherous net of political deceit with it's compounded rules and regulations designed to confuse and intimidate "the little man" into conformance, and therefore less likely to observe the traitorous aberrations of government. A government with 20,000 lawyers on the payroll has to be suspect of it's intentions! Every candidate for political office in Washington states with what we now realize is nothing but BS, that he will work to reduce the size of government – but instead contributes to the further bloating, inefficiency, and higher cost of government by becoming a party to more and more politically generated "programs" that wastes taxpayer money! Perplexing is the operative word as to why our political leaders cannot be honest and forthright instead of stooping to secrecy, deceit, and betrayal of Real American citizens!

Fully ten per cent or more of real Americans face a tragic and desperate future every day, having been condemned to a miserable existence and forced to live in inhuman squalor conditions while our politicians live a life of luxury and ignoring the tragic circumstances of millions of Real Americans.

Why is this? It's the same age old story – the poor and desperate have no political clout and get the short end of the stick – it's that simple. The poor will always be in the same caste system -that's right, America does have a caste system and what's more, supported and perpetuated by the callous attitude and actions of a majority of our elected representatives.

The American dream is being turned into a nightmare for the average Real American family who are being denied THEIR RIGHTS of Life, Liberty and the Pursuit of Happiness by a majority of our politicians in state and federal governments pursuing a Politically Correct posture and stupidity in providing BILLIONS of Taxpayer Dollars to Illegal Immigrant Criminals! It can only be said this is a betrayal of constituent confidence and trust of the highest order! Allegiance to foreigners by those elected to represent Real Americans in need is in effect a publicly demonstrated contempt for their constituents and betrayal of America!

Several thousand persons die each year from heat strokes, suffocation, freezing and starvation, strictly due to the contempt afforded them by our political parties. One could perhaps draw the conclusion this is criminal neglect by default. However, it is a different ball game when examining treatment and privileges for the illegal criminal immigrants running rampant all over America. These Illegal (criminal) hordes are afforded all the privileges at no cost - free of charge - that working Americans have been paying into the Government Treasury as FICA taxes for their entire working careers! In addition, - if you can believe this – hundreds of police forces all over America have been ordered not to ask obviously suspicious persons if they are in America legally. This is unbelievable and emphasizes the ignorant yellow belly idiots who have wormed their way in positions of authority through lying and brown nosing! Again, these people are traitors to America and need to be tarred and feathered and given a ride out of town!

The law is being usurped by no guts officials who are breaking the law themselves and should be forced to resign their position and prosecuted for treason against America for aiding and abetting Illegal Criminal Invaders! The word "Illegal" once meant "Against the Law" – but apparently Webster's dictionary has been amended by scared politicians to mean : "The Right to Be Criminals"

The majority of politicians have for many years betrayed the interest and welfare of the very people who elected and put them in office. As a matter of interest to many people, the United States political system was designed after the ancient Romans and held its first session on March 4, 1789. However, since the 1950's, our representative type of government has deteriorated from a belief in a Higher Being, the welfare of America and it's citizens regardless of opinions and criticism from outside sources to one of total abandonment of American principles! It appears from newspaper and television reporting that the majority of it's sessions are consumed attempting to discredit the other party by personal insults, fake charges, outright lying about the other party and a Political Correctness posture in foreign affairs and Illegal Immigration The urgent business of America's survival is put on hold! One version of interpreting the meaning of Political Correctness is : cowardice, yellow belly, and no guts which in turn means doing nothing while standing directly on the fence so as to appear innocent. Many of these spoiled, selfish and detestable offspring of the true and Real Americans of the post World War II era have wormed their way into politics and sent America on the path to collapse. "Spare the rod and raise a traitor" Political Correctness as practiced to perfection by most politicians for personal gain and ducking responsibility, has succeeded in eroding millions of jelly headed mentalities in our present day decadent society to the point of accepting the teachings of those who seek to destroy the American values of the past!

Wishful thinking and running from the problem won't get it! This is a guaranteed certainty of America's decline into failure and the Genocide of Real Americans unless our yellow bellied elected doughbrain politicians all over America stand up and be counted as Americans for America. What we have here is a group of supposedly grown men elected by the people to support the original ideas and convictions of our courageous forefathers who, instead, continue acting like demented juveniles. The United States of America is being betrayed by many top Politically Correct politicians and are imitated as role models by mindless idiot school system officials, county commissions, city commissions, college professors, regents and presidents, unqualified teachers, (thousands of these), many state governors, and our college students are now becoming traitors to America through the seditionist ramblings of sick professors. The activities of these people are a cancer on the American way of life and the pity of it is they are so stupid they fail to realize when America collapses they go down also. The unbelievable ignorance of these supposedly educated and intelligent people is mind staggering. There seems to be a contagious brain disease by a large percentage of American multi millionaires, movie actor airheads and certain television personalities that America must conform to the opinion of the rest of the world and cower and beg for their approval. These jelly bean brains are totally without a clue that they and their ilk will be the first victims of the smothering hordes of mongrels from all over the world -especially Illegal Immigrant Criminals when they take over America –and they will if the present un-American scared tactics of the majority our gutless so-called leaders continues!

This waterlogged, brainwashed mentality is the absolute opposite of what was once America; an America that stood up to all challenges with no apologies and whipped the crap of any who tried to change us. This is America; we do it our way – you don't like it – too bad! Now, with Political Correctness permeating the heads of weak minded pinheads in America, including an alarming number of our government officials, we have an undeniable decay of the American Society which if not turned around will result in a collapse of our nation and guarantee America's collapse into oblivion! (See tables below). Once we challenged all comers – now we apologize! America is now at the average survival time limit of historical nations that were called democracies and is exactly on the same time track toward extinction as the ancient civilizations of Rome, Carthage, and Greece! History is repeating itself again and even the majority of our dumb leaders are too rotten to bring America back on track by responsible conservative independent thinking. Are they puppets of foreign nations or One World proponents? Recommended reading: "The Fall of Rome!"

A nation cannot survive when the citizens have no morals, no pride, no patriotism, do not participate in government, sex is king, rape, murder and death is ignored, judges run rampant with their insane decisions, graft and corruption at highest levels of government and industry, and the most important function of living is to "Let the Good Times Roll".

A trusting constituent would believe an elected official would remember his lying rhetoric before election and ensure he followed up on his promises to his trusting constituents. Let's not kid ourselves, his lies are the last thing he intends to honor – more important activities are consuming his interest! He has spread his BS all over the district populace and been elected; So, Now To The Good Life!

Oath required by the Constitution and by Law to be taken by Government officials when taking office:

I,_A,B_, do solemnly swear or (affirm) that I will support and defend the Constitution of the United States against all enemies, foreign and domestic, that I will bear true faith and allegiance to the same, that I take this obligation freely, without any mental reservation or purpose of evasion; and that I will well and faithfully discharge the office of which I am about to enter

So Help Me God!

Lying and betrayal of a sworn oath on the Bible is an impeachable offense! This applies to any and all government officials from President to Congressmen!

Various politicians are constantly whining about the cost of removing the Illegal Invaders physically from the United States which is sickening. Again, these are supposedly grown intelligent adults but from their misguided, scared and ignorant excuses only one fact is absolute : A large percentage of our elected politicians are betraying the trust of the Real American citizens by approving subsidies for foreign Illegal Invaders – the reason: No Guts (they're scared of morons) and turning a blind eye to the eventual result of smothering hordes of ignorant Illegal Criminals swarming into America. The cost of rounding up and removing these Illegal Criminals will be no more – if as much – than the annual costs now coming out of the United States Treasury and directly from Real American's pockets to pay for subsidizing these criminals. Providing Medicare and Medicaid, Food Stamps, Daycare, School Facilities, (totally wasted expense and effort) Clothes and Prison Space for criminal activities by Illegal Criminals for just one year will pay for transporting these invaders back to Mexico and building an impregnable wall to prevent further destruction of America! The recent demonstrations in California and the no guts response of the Governor's office provided a real life insight into what these ignorant and filthy excuses for human beings have in store for the United States of America.

The criminal leaders of Mexican outlaw organizations have openly stated their objective and purpose is to trample all of America's traditions into the dust by sheer masses of numbers, kill Gringos, have millions of babies, get voting control and take over America!! Birth control responsibility is totally ignored and further emphasizes their ignorance and stupidity. By 2040 (or sooner) if these illegal invaders are not removed, this irresponsible horde will be 25 – 40 percent of the population in America due to the direct and treasonous actions of the gutless no-action policy of our so-called leaders! Who will be President, Vice – President, United States Senators and House of Representatives in America when this happens? Many have wondered about Vicente' Fox and his part in the smothering hordes who rush into America virtually unhindered! Texas, California, New Mexico and Arizona are apparently controlled by Mexican Illegal Criminals now with cowardly officials afraid to arrest and deport them. Where are the Governors and police officials - are they being told to layoff? Confrontations have demonstrated the cowardice of mayors and city councils in many cities where demonstrations by these half-witted uneducated idiot Illegal Criminals have sent the city officials scurrying for cover like frightened rats – is this no guts or Political pressure from certain elements of our weak government?

Recent events at the Mexican border have produced a cloud of distrust over the justice system in America. These officials, sworn to protect America against all enemies, foreign and domestic, have apparently fallen into the Political Correctness trap – either intentionally or mistakenly – the effect is the same – and sent the wrong message to enemies of America. Several loyal Representatives,Tom Tancredo, Dana Rohrabacher and Duncan Hunter have had the guts to speak out and condemn these official actions which in their opinion leave a strong impression of intimidation of U.S. citizens, accommodation of foreign criminals, Police State tactics and Kangaroo Courts. To paraphrase: "A criminal by any other name is still a criminal! Underneath any sugar coating of official immunity remains the same piece of crap!

From evidence supported by the news media it certainly appears the large majority of our leaders are total Wimps. It also appears some of their traitorous decisions concerning Illegal Criminals are dictated by lobbyists for big business. Why is this? : This makes it possible for corporations to pay starvation threshold wages to ignorant Illegal Criminals and pay hundreds of millions of dollars in "Bonuses" to top racketeering executives. This is the epitome of greed and complete disregard for REAL AMERICANS who are the genuine backbone of American industry! To repeat a previous statement:

There is a no nation on this earth more corrupt than the United States of America!

Listed below is the actual and real life fact that, instead of saving consumers money, Real American taxpayers are saddled with the following support mechanisms designed especially for Illegal Immigrants which continues to degrade quality of life for all Americans:

Let's look at for example, an illegal alien with a wife and five children. This is the typical illegal alien family and explains why there are millions of deadly Illegal Immigrants eager to cross the border and kill if necessary to suck up these benefits:

1. He takes a job for $5.00 or $6.00/ hour.
2. At that wage, with six dependents, he pays no income tax, yet at the end of the year, if he files an Income Tax Return, he gets an "earned income credit" of up to $3,200 free.
3. He qualifies for Section 8 housing and subsidized rent.
4. He qualifies for food stamps.
5. He qualifies for free (no deductible, no co-pay) health care.
6. His children get free breakfasts and lunches at school.
7. He requires bilingual teachers and books.
8. He qualifies for relief from high energy bills.
9. If they are or become, aged, blind or disabled, they qualify for SSI.
10. Once qualified for SSI they can qualify for Medicare.
11. All of this is at that taxpayer's expense.
12. He doesn't worry about car insurance, life insurance, or homeowners insurance.
13. Taxpayers provide Spanish language signs, bulletins and printed material.
14. He and his family receive the equivalent of $20.00 to $30.00 /hour in benefits.

15. Working Americans are lucky to have $5.00 or $6.00/ hour left after paying their portion to support the Illegal Aliens.

16. The American taxpayers also pay for increased <u>crime, graffiti and trash clean-up</u>.

Items 1 through 16 are what our so-called political leaders have in store for America! In fact, at this point in time the American taxpayer is already subsidizing $11,000,000,000 to $13,000,000,000 (Billion) on the present hordes swamping this nation. It boggles the imagination at what the cost will be in the future with the continued apathetic and pathetic attitude of our cowardly so-called political leaders!

It's time to call out the National Guard or Regular Militia to round up Illegal Immigrant Criminals and load them on trucks for a trip back to Mexico before Real Americans are forced to do it to save America and their families from destruction. The majority of Real Americans are wondering why Governor Arnold Schwarzenegger (The Movie Hero?) of California failed to stand up for America and crush the Mexican anti-American demonstration by arresting rioters flying the American Flag upside down UNDER the lousy Mexican flag? – The idea behind treasonous demonstrations such as this is to suppress and intimidate with massive numbers since they have found that COWARDS, COWARDS, COWARDS are running America.

An assessment of the actions of our political "masters" (they seem to be convinced they are) leaves no doubt at this point in time that Real Americans will have to defend THEIR rights to avoid being swept aside by Illegal Immigrant hordes dropping babies all over America's landscape and smothering the nation. They state publicly that Arizona, Texas, New Mexico and California belong to Mexico and will take this territory back. Is this for real? Mexicans are for Mexicans - there will be no assimilation. Spanish is their language – they have said many times already - No English! You can bet on it unless our Politically Correct cowardly politicians stand up for America and live up to their sworn oaths! Hopefully, our cowardly leaders will resolve this national disgrace before survival violence occurs!

Number One in this traitorous group is the Politically Correct government officials who are apparently scared out of their wits, desperately attempting to figure a way to solve a problem of their own creation! There are only two options: One is to hold out a welcoming hand to the Illegal Criminal invaders and give away America to barbarians, or Two : Plan and execute physical removal from American soil, all Illegal Immigrant Criminals even if this requires calling out the U.S. Army. Loud screams of protests for all over the world may be heard but who cares – America is America - not Mexico! After contemplation, which would be the worst fate : 1. To face a angry American public bent on revenge or, 2. Deal with Mr. Bush?

Next is Arnold Schwarzenegger who decided to ignore this direct subversive public rioting by Hispanics rather than calling out the National Guard to do whatever necessary to stop the dastardly contempt shown by these ignorant criminals for the United States when they arrogantly flew the American Flag upside down under the Mexican flag! Trashing of America will be the result of occupation by foreign Illegal Immigrant Invaders while our scared disloyal "Public Servants" stand idly by and indicate their stamp of approval when they vacillate and whine! This American? has stated publicly he will provide all the subsistence needed by (as he so unbelievably says)" poor illegal criminals". California is even now being forced to attempt to build one (1) new school every day (impossible) to attempt to keep up with the overwhelming demands of the criminal invader elements that have just at this point bankrupted 6 hospitals in California and 77 medical facilities in America! What does this aberration of a normal mentality hold in store for California citizens? More and more taxes and less and less quality of life! Education in schools is steadily deteriorating and casting America farther and farther behind in competition with standards and progress with even some third world countries.

Next is our own President -George Bush – who, in the opinion of Real Americans, has slapped them in the face with his obvious indifference for the continuing influx of millions of Illegal Invaders from Mexico – and continuing to lower quality of life for all working Real Americans while the rich get richer – by underhanded design! (The story is he had a Mexican Nanny). Big Business calls the shots and controls the government! They are the upper crust – you, the real Americans are the burned toast! Now you know exactly where you stand in the pecking order of political influence – with the bottom of politician's filthy rotten boots on your neck!

As stated previously and bears repeating is this: Political Correctness (a synonym for gutlessness) is destroying America and sending this once great nation to the graveyard of betrayed ideologies by those entrusted with the care and security of their country.

Birth control responsibility by Illegal Criminals is totally ignored and further emphasizes their ignorance and stupidity. By 2040 this irresponsible horde will be 25-40 percent of the population in America thanks to the direct and traitorous actions of many of our so-called leaders top to bottom!

President Theodore Roosevelt said in 1907:

"In the first place we should insist that if the immigrant who comes here in good faith becomes an American and assimilates himself to us, he shall be treated on an exact equality with everyone else, for it is an outrage to discriminate against any such man because of creed, or birthplace, or origin. But this is predicated upon the man's becoming in very fact an American, and nothing but an American...There can be no divided allegiance here. Any man who says he is an American, but something else also, isn't an American at all. We have room for but one flag, the American flag, and this excludes the red flag, which symbolizes all wars against liberty and civilization, just as much as it excludes any foreign flag of a nation to which we are hostile...We have room for but one language here, and that is the English language...and we have room for but one sole loyalty and that is a loyalty to the American people."

America could benefit immensely from a president such as Theodore Roosevelt. The travesty America now faces due to underhanded yellow traitors would never been remotely tolerated.

Perhaps the majority of those so-called Americans in the House and Senate should read the article below written by an anonymous Real American and act upon these patriotic truths, or is it expecting too much of our Elected Representatives – who are supposed to vote as the people of this nation believe – not to suit their own fanciful, mistaken and traitorous ideas:

Immigrants, Not Americans Must Adapt

"I am tired of this nation worrying about whether we are offending some individual or their culture. Since the terrorist attacks on September 11, we have experienced a surge in patriotism by the majority of Americans. However, the dust from the attacks had barely settled when the Politically Correct (Especially the A.C.L.U.) crowd began complaining about the possibility that our patriotism was offending others. I am not against immigration, nor do I hold a grudge against anyone who is seeking a better life by coming to America legally! Our population is almost entirely comprised of descendants of immigrants – legal immigrants! However, there are a few things that those who have recently come to our country and also some who were born here need to understand. This idea of America being a multi-cultural community has only served to dilute our sovereignty and our national identity. As Americans, we have our own culture, our own society, our own language and our own lifestyle. This culture has been developed over centuries of struggles, trials, and victories by millions of men and women who have sought freedom. We speak English, not Spanish, Arabic, Chinese, Japanese, Russian, or any other language. Therefore, if you wish to become part of our society, learn the language! "In God we trust" is our national motto! This is not some Christian right wing, political slogan. We adopted this motto because Christian men and women, on Christian principles, founded this nation, and this is clearly documented. It is certainly appropriate to display it on the walls of our schools. If God offends you then I suggest you consider another part of the world as your new home, because God is part of our culture! If Stars and Stripes offend you, or you don't like Uncle Sam, then you should immediately move to another part of this planet. We are happy with our culture and have no desire to change, and we really don't care how you did things where you came from. This is **our country**, our land and our lifestyle. Our first amendment to the Constitution of the United States of America gives every CITIZEN the right to express his opinion and we will allow you every opportunity to do so. But, once you are done complaining, burning our flag, whining and griping about our pledge, our national motto, or our way of life, I highly encourage you to take advantage of one other great American freedom: THE RIGHT TO LEAVE!"

It is a pity the Patriotic beliefs and convictions expressed by the anonymous writer above are not shared by the majority of our so-called political leaders and judges who are giving America away to complaining foreigners and illegal immigrant criminals. It seems that any foreigner (legal or illegal) can take issue with our laws, our rules and regulation, our historical values, appear in a supposed court of law with a greedy corrupt attorney who has no character, and get some unqualified lousy American judge declare the law and/or regulation illegal or being against the foreigner's rights. According to the performance of our elected political leaders and many courts it seems everybody in this faulted and decadent system hunkers down to the A.C.L.U. It appears all the A.C. L.U. has to do is demand anything patriotic be removed, destroyed, rewritten to their satisfaction, stated in a Politically Correct language of their choosing and PRESTO!-America is castrated again and again by legal infirm minds ready to do their bidding. The treachery to traditional American values has extended to accommodating foreign invaders in Texas, California, Arizona, and New Mexico by installing street signs, direction signs and building directions in Spanish! Is this America – YES – but not for long! Most of our scared so-called leaders are so intimidated by illegal criminals smothering America that they have surrendered and reduced to wringing their hands in abject cowardice and indecision except to whine and offer some version of Amnesty. Replacement with people of character, dedication and guts is sorely needed.

Hopefully, these people will be remembered at election time by American voters and will give them the old heave-ho out of office- while there is still a chance to save America! Take heed at the implication of the tables below and names of Senators that voted Medicare for Illegal Criminals, and voted against making English the official language of the United States of America!

William Shakespeare in the famous play "Hamlet" said : "To be or not to be, that is the question, whether 'tis nobler in the mind to bear the slings and arrows of outrageous fortune, or to take arms against a sea of troubles and by opposing, end them."

The American people are now being kicked in the teeth and stabbed in the back by the careless, indifferent, disloyal and deceitful secrecy and subterfuge by many of their so-called political leaders. The sobering fact is the realization that America is and will continue to be, swamped and overrun by ignorant, murdering socially irresponsible Illegal Hispanics and other criminals until Real Americans are no longer in charge of the great nation their forefathers and subsequent generations developed and died for to insure a free nation for future generations and survival of the species.

Now, "Yankee" ingenuity survival is being sacrificed on the altar of treasonous political indecision, fear, and procrastination instead of determined, prompt and effective permanent action to suppress the invaders! Who cares what other people, other nations or the ACLU says? Give 'em the third digit – this is America, OUR country – so back off and stick it! What should be the reaction of Real Americans be if our so-called political leaders betray their oaths of office? Should they sit idly by while America is consumed by irresponsible gangs of foreign illegal criminals or by opposing, defend and assert THEIR rights so frequently violated by legal shenanigans and usurpation of power by many cowardly and indifferent politicians in the highest and

18

lowest offices! Failure to defend their legal rights as Americans in the face of illegal criminal takeover is to be faced with eventual genocide. Most politicians, will, out of sheer cowardice and ignorance cast aspersions and jeer at a prediction of America's collapse if illegal criminal immigrants are not deported and immediately-by whatever means necessary! However, numbers don't lie like most politicians!

The once great Roman society failed under the same exact conditions as is occurring in America due to so-called "superior beings" (politicians) living it up ("Let the Good Times Roll)" and ignoring the threat from within. This problem could have been solved years ago if our so-called political leaders had been restraining G. Bush and serving Real America citizens per their sworn oath instead of their own selfish interest! Traitorous activity by politicians reinforces the truth of the historical observation "Nero fiddled while Rome burned." Burned and destroyed by IMMIGRANTS who outsmarted their "superior politicians".

Again, it is perplexing and disturbing when supposed intelligent Americans fall victim and bow and cringe in response to rotten philosophies propagated by enemies of the United States!

The physical removal of Illegal Criminals from the property of the United States of America can be, and should be accomplished as follows if America is to be rescued and saved from extinction by smothering hordes of irresponsible illegal immigrant criminals who vow to take back Texas, Arizona, New Mexico and California and are already taking over in the face of cowardly so-called leaders:

1. Establish necessary temporary detention centers across America – there are already many of these under construction for reasons presently unknown?

2. Issue a national order for all illegal persons to report to the nearest detention center for processing and identification within one month.

3. Penalty for those refusing or ignoring the order will be arrest, prosecution, detention for five years in a prison camp with fences and tents and deportation.

19

4. Deportation can be an ongoing function as processing progresses.

Now, here comes the screaming protests, not only from dumb organizations supporting Illegal Criminal Invaders, the ACLU (What's New), Subversive Mexican Organizations which should be closed down (Our yellow belly legal system only persecutes Americans), Big Business racketeers, certain traitorous Banking Institutions and bleeding hearts with diarrhea of the mouth and constipation of the brain.

The success of this operation is dependent on the will and guts of our political establishment. Do they care about the future of America and Real Americans or are they dedicated pawns to big business and willing to destroy America thru refusing to eliminate the irresponsible and certain over population siphoning off all America's resources? As prognosticated earlier, there will be loud protests that the cost of an effort such as this will be prohibitive. This is typical political BS crapola and actual cost would be no more than two years of present giveaway programs by our so-called political leaders and include also a 700 mile border fence!

This is the only practical method of dealing with and handling a situation that has been festering and fomenting for years and ignored by our so-called leaders. Now, It's too late to sweep this abdication of a sworn duty under the rug of deceit! To do otherwise and procrastinate is to increase exponentially, the certain breakdown of American society and war in America's streets!

Below is direct confirmation of the contempt by our so-called leaders for Real American citizens and their families whose lives will be impacted with a lower quality of life by this traitorous action! This is the official recorded list of United States Senators who voted to provide Social Security benefits for illegal criminal invaders – 12,000,000 – 18,000,000 of them - and graphically illustrates the uncaring, mistaken and Political Correctness actions of a large percentage of trusted law makers.

Voted To Give Social Security To Illegal Immigrants

Alaska:Stevens (R

Arizona:McCain (R) ******

Arkansas:Lincoln (D)Pryor (D)

California:Boxer (D)Feinstein D

Colorado:Salazar:(D)

Connecticut:Dodd:(D)   Lieberman:(D)

Delaware:Biden (D)   Carper:(D)

Florida:Martinez (R)

Hawaii:Akaka (D)Inouye (D

Illinois:Durbin (D)
Obama:(D) *****

Indiana:Bayh (D)   Lugar:(R)

Iowa: Harkin (D)

Kansas: Brownback (R)

Louisiana: Landrieu (D)

Maryland:

Mikulski (D):   Sarbanes (D)

Massachusetts: Kennedy (D) Kerry (D)

Montana: Baucus (D)

Nebraska:Hagel (R)

Nevada:Reid (D)

New Jersey:Lautenberg (D):Menendez (D)

New Mexico:Bingaman (D)

New York:Clinton *****(D):   Schumer (D)

North Dakota: Dorgan (D)

Ohio:DeWine (R)   Voinovich(R)

Oregon:Wyden (D)

Pennsylvania:Specter (R)

Rhode Island:Chafee (R): Reed (D)

South Carolina: Graham (R)

South Dakota: Johnson (D)

Vermont: Jeffords (I):   Leahy (D)

Washington: Cantwell (D):Murray (D)

West Virginia: Rockefeller(D),

Wisconsin: Feingold (D): Kohl (D)

****** **And these three want to be president???**

This is the ultimate insult to Real Americans who have been and will continue to pay FICA taxes into the Federal Treasury for years under threat of jail time to support FREE Social Security for ILLEGAL CRIMINALS!

The United States Senate has 100 Members and the House of Representatives has 435 members and most of these (except a very few patriots) have a very dim view of the intelligence of voters. The general opinion of most Real Americans polled is that the U.S. Senate is by far the most saturated and disgraced by those who are intending, because of cowardice and personal rottenness, to betray

America through a treasonous vote for Amnesty. The sad and at the same time angering abandonment of the people's wishes by these liars is the stark and rude awakening fact that we, the people, have been snookered by the Mr. Jekyll and Mr. Hyde personalities elected by trusting voters! One wonders what would be the response if en masse, these so-called lousy representatives of the people were asked: "are you proud of betraying the Real Americans who placed total faith in you to respond to their wishes?" A personal poll of 100 Real Americans were asked to compare the list of Senators below who voted for Amnesty to Benedict Arnold. Ninety - seven percent replied "The same" , "Just as Bad", "worse, because there are so many"

Now is the time to get MAD AS HELL and let these traitors among the Real Americans feel the venom of your bite!

Remember the Merriam- Webster definition of Traitor? :

"One who betrays another's trust or is false to an obligation or duty."

VOTING FOR AMNESTY FOR CRIMINALS QUALIFIES AS A PERFECT MATCH TO THE DEFINITION OF TRAITOR. (This also qualifies for impeachment!).

Let's take a moment to repeat the oath of office for Senators of the United States of America and see how their performance matches their sworn statement:

Oath required by the Constitution and by Law to be taken by Government officials when taking office:

I,_A,B_, do solemnly swear or (affirm) that I will support and defend the Constitution of the United States against all enemies, foreign and domestic, that I will bear true faith and allegiance to the same, that I take this obligation freely, without any mental reservation or purpose of evasion; and that I will well and faithfully discharge the office of which I am about to enter.

So Help Me God!

Even the sloppiest and most liberal interpretation of the oath above cannot help but point out with dramatic certainty the direct intentional betrayal of their sworn oath of office. There is no evading the truth of what these people have committed against their own nation. They swore on the bible to defend America against all enemies foreign and domestic but have crawled under their respective desks to hide from their sworn oath to protect America and Americans.

For years we have been hearing the whining from government officials that Social Security is on the brink of failure due to lack of funds. So; where is the extra BILLIONS coming from to support 12,000,000 – 18,000,000 ILLEGAL ALIEN CRIMINALS (existing total) with FREE Social Security that Real Americans are FORCED to pay or go to jail! This is America?

Taxes on Real Americans will be increased! In fact, at this writing new Tax Bills are being written in an attempt to pay for the dereliction of duty to hard working Real Americans by many of our so-called leaders.

Thomas Jefferson said: (This says it all).

"We must not let our rulers load us with perpetual debt. We must make our election between economy and liberty or profusion and servitude. If we run into such debt, as that we must be taxed in our meat and in our drink, in our necessaries and our comforts, in our labors and our amusements, for our calling and our creeds... [we will] have no time to think, no means of calling our miss-managers to account but be glad to obtain subsistence by hiring ourselves to rivet their chains on the necks of our fellow-sufferers... And this is the tendency of all human governments. A departure from principle in one instance becomes a precedent for [another]... till the bulk of society is reduced to be mere automatons of misery... And the fore-horse of this frightful team is public debt. Taxation follows that, and in its train wretchedness, deceit and oppression."

There is no additional source of Social Security funding available except to raise FICA payroll taxes of American citizens and other taxes such as income, gasoline, alcohol, tobacco, automobiles, movie theaters, and excise taxes. A gutless move by our so-called leaders such as this will further lower the quality of living for lower and middle income Americans and will force real Americans to pay more taxes for a lower quality of life. Not so for our so-called leaders - federal and state – just vote themselves a juicy raise at taxpayer expense and life is great and good! This being so, a look down the road at Social Security will reveal at least a 30 -35 percent minimum increase in payroll deductions to you, a loyal Real American, due to ILLEGAL IMMIGRANT CRIMINALS and their totally ignorant birthrate irresponsibility. A minimum of Five to Six children is the average for these people who have no respect for America and quality of life. (Sort of like dogs). Multiply 12,000,000 -18,000,000 Illegal Criminals by 5 or 6 and in one breath it becomes tragically obvious what will happen to REAL AMERICANS and their future! There is no other patriotic method or moral procedural action by our so-called leaders except to REMOVE these 12,000,000 -18,000,000 Illegal Immigrant Criminals from the United States of America which is for American citizens! If they do not, American citizens have no choice; for the sake of their own livelihood, a reasonable quality of life and future for their families, but to take whatever measures necessary! It's time to get rid of all the gutless traitors in our midst and the need is obvious to vote them out of office immediately in favor of Patriotic Americans as the only resort short of violence. Free Social Security and other free assistance for Illegal Criminals is the most outrageous action ever perpetrated by our so-called leaders against Real American citizens - all American citizens!

Shown below is another disgraceful and traitorous action by many U.S. Senators indicating how they feel about America. This is the official recorded U.S. Senate vote on making English the official language of the United States of America. Is this the type of people we want to be our leaders and to guide America? How much more obvious can it be that the "No" votes are for the Illegal hordes swamping America! It seems that for many of our so-called leaders,

Political Correctness is a chosen way of life and to be a stand up Real American is unthinkable and a disparaging insult to foreign invaders! To paraphrase "You are for Real American principles or you are against Real American principles!

Voted Against Making English The Official Language

Akaka (D-HI)	Cantwell (D-WA
Bayh (D-IN)	Schumer (D-NY)
Biden (D-DE)	Stabenow (D-MI)
Bingaman (D-NM)	Inouye-D-HI
Boxer (D-CA))	Kennedy-D-MA Kerry-D-MA
Clinton (D-NY)** Dayton (D-MN)	Harkin-D-IA
Dodd (D-CT)	Dayton-D-MN
Domenici (R-NM)	Cantwell-D-WA
Durbin (D-IL)	Lautenburg-D-NJ
Feingold (D-WI) Kohl-D-WI	Wyden (D-OR
Feinstein (D-CA)	Mikulski (D-MD) Sarbanes-(D-MD)
Leahy (D-VT) Jeffords-D-VT	Murray (D-WA)
Levin (D-MI)	**Obama (D-IL)****
Lieberman (D-CT)	Reed (D-RI)
Menendez (D-NJ)	Reid (D-NV) Salazar (D-CO)

And these two want to be president? What they deserve is a massive and resounding "No" vote!

 National Security in America is a disgraceful and traitorous cover up to lull the American people into a sense of complacency. It's the same old story of political hacks back scratching and favoritism – the "good 'ole boy" syndrome and will come to light when America is attacked again!

Obviously, the tragic events of 9/11 has faded and grown dim in the memory of the political hierarchy to a unimportant role in regard to preparation for certain future attacks by terrorists. Our so called leaders have once again shown their lack of concern for anyone but themselves by appointing experienced practitioners of BS to positions of authority and leadership to supposedly protect America from terrorist attacks. Instead of choosing active or retired military leaders and strategists who have an undeniable handle on warfare and the enemy and how to plan and neutralize the threat, what we get is "somebody's buddy" who doesn't know proper procedures from a hole in the ground to protect America! This is typical political shenanigans. America is facing callous and murderous enemies and the status quo is "steady as she goes". The situation of no cooperation between the FBI, CIA, Secret Service and other agencies is traitorous to the welfare of the United States of America and is the total failure of the our despicable political leadership in America!

Terrorists can attack the United States at any time with almost total impunity. They are biding their time to prepare a truly horrible and destructive event that will wreck America and our weak will to fight back. Political Correctness is destroying American's integrity and courage. When – not if – we are attacked again America will collapse like a house of cards – remember - "Let The Good Times Roll" is the national theme today with two thirds of our future political prospects being totally unaware, gullible and insensitive to America's plight in favor of the good life – totally irresponsible parasitic citizens. This again is a result of the lousy example setting for our society by our political so-called leaders! It appears that the present policy of these so-called leaders is and has been for years now – Political Correctness, the most treacherous, and insidious genocide weapon ever conceived. Political Correctness is a terminal mindless and gutless disease designed to destroy the spirit and mind of the citizens of America and creating puppets of millions of the pinheaded "Good Time Charlies" who are sucking it up hook line and sinker – with the full cooperation of most of America's so-called leaders who are the primary propagators of this mind altering disease!

James Monroe (Fifth President of the United States) said:

"{In a Republic} it is not the people themselves who make the decisions, but those they have chosen to stand in their place"

Once upon a long time ago, America was a Republic, now we have a Democracy which is a curse of the devil on Real Americans wherein the stupid, the ignorant, Illegal Immigrant Criminals, the loafers and the disloyal traitors can control America's destiny! This alone is tantamount to the "kiss of death" for America. For a nation to survive, those chosen to stand up for loyal trusting citizens must have integrity, knowledge, and the courage to speak the truth!

Where are they?

Thomas Jefferson said :

A Democracy is nothing more than mob rule where fifty-one percent of the people may take away the rights of the other forty-nine!

Again:

President John Adams said:

Democracy never lasts long. It soon wastes, exhausts and murders itself. There was never a democracy that did not commit suicide! April 15, 1814

Many questions are being raised as to why George Bush did not act while Governor of Texas and now as President of the United States to stem the flow of hordes of illegal so-called immigrants from Mexico! The visits to Mexico have raised eyebrows in puzzlement as the Illegal Immigrant hordes continued to breeze into America and border agents have their hands tied. The silent answer to this question is deafening!

This is the perfect environment and opportunity for terrorists to infiltrate into the United States. By Federal decree our border guards are told to practice POLITICAL CORRECTNESS when confronting these CRIMINALS. Even more disgusting is the Federal decree that the totally ineffective number of Nation Guard personnel on the border cannot have weapons – is this insanely stupid or what? Our political leaders are preoccupied with Political Correctness as an escape mechanism from responsible actions against our enemies - enemies that will chop off your head, mutilate, rape, torture and kill women and children and laugh! The majority of our so-called political leaders seem to be totally unaware, uncaring and totally ignoring the certain future disastrous collapse of our society if all immigration is not halted and enforced effectively for at least five years! The Statue of Liberty is no longer applicable to America and should be melted down into parts for the border fence! However, this will not happen until our so-called political leaders have the guts to discard Political Correctness and stand up for America.-The opinion of America by the rest of the world is born of jealously and hate- and our so-called political leaders are remiss and lacking integrity as usual in not standing up and tell all of them to kiss off! Immigration laws are in desperate need of modifying and being enforced. America cannot afford more millions of people when all around us is the evidence of overpopulation versus more murders, rapes, poverty, infrastructure destruction and wasteful consumption of natural resources, floods, foreign criminal gangs and lack of funds and personnel. Most of our lawmakers across the nation are old and mentally decrepit and abandoning America in favor of self-gratification and throwing Real Americans to the wolves!

Now, let's take a look at those countries that hate us and how they vote in the United Nations and also the part played by the United States Senate and House of Representatives in this debacle by continuing to giveaway -literally throwing away -multiple BILLIONS of TAXPAYER dollars each and every year:

The United States gives $13,000,000,000 to $18,000,000,000 (that's BILLION) tax dollars in direct so- called Foreign Aid annually. The United States giveaway is above and beyond the single most generous benefactor of the United Nations, and most of the billions of dollars goes to third-world dictators. In addition $2.4,000,000,000 is donated to the United Nations for operating expenses.

This amount is 25% of the United Nations budget. In addition, the United States also gives another $1.4 billion tax dollars to United Nations' programs and agencies. The American taxpayers fund more for the United Nations than ALL of the other 177 member nations COMBINED.

What most Americans do not realize is that the vast majority of the recipients of US Foreign Aid routinely vote against the wishes of the United States in the UN at an average rate of 74%. In other words, of the $13 to $18 billion tax dollars invested in direct Foreign Aid only about $3.5 to 4.5 billion went to support people who endorsed American initiatives or causes. A staggering $9.8 plus billion tax dollars went to causes and people who were and are in open and direct opposition to the United States' interests and objectives.

Below are the actual voting records of various Arabic/Islamic States which are recorded in both the US State Department and United Nations records.

Kuwait votes against the United States 67% of the time.

Qatar votes against the United States 67% of the time.

Morocco votes against the United States 70% of the time.

United Arab Emirates votes against the US.. 70% of the time.

Jordan votes against the United States 71% of the time.

Tunisia votes against the United States 71% of the time.

Saudi Arabia votes against the United States 73% of the time.

Yemen votes against the United States 74% of the time

Algeria votes against the United States 74% of the time.

Oman votes against the United States 74% of the time

Sudan votes against the United States 75% of the time.

Pakistan votes against the United States 75% of the time.

Libya votes against the United States 76% of the time.

This information alone should infuriate Americans forced to live and exist – that's the appropriate word - EXIST –on the disgusting penny-pinching handouts by the political shenanigans of our rotten political system.

Yet it seems there is no problem providing multi billions of American Taxpayer's hard earned money as so called Foreign Aid to lousy no good rotten corrupt countries that hate America! The governments are free to spend this "free gift' as they like with no accounting supervision by the United States.

This should infuriate all Americans struggling to get by from payday to payday. This is the real world and what this book is all about –traitorous Americans with no guts destroying America!

It is obvious to everyone with only a smattering of intelligence that this is a direct insult to all taxpayers in the United States and represents a total lack of respect for the source of these billions of dollars – YOU, the overwhelmed taxpayer. This is more evidence that all you represent to our so-called leaders is only an inexhaustible source of money to attempt to buy friendship which any person with half - a- brain knows is impossible. This wasted expensive effort in trying to show the world what wonderful generous humanitarians they are is in stark contrast to giving nothing to thousands of loyal American citizens dying of starvation, heat strokes, freezing, multiple diseases and abandonment. The old saying that "Charity begins at home" has never been truer. It's all about money and demonstration of power, and if this travesty continues our mistaken politicians will bring America to her knees.

We continue to hear poor mouthing platitudes concerning the desperate financial condition of the United States of America in continuing to finance Medicare and Medicaid by appointed liars from many of our so-called political leaders. We need some of these liars and thieves that have been stealing the country blind for years to have the guts to tell us where the Billions of Dollars are coming from to finance the Illegal Criminals FREE Medicare, Transportation, Schooling (Rotten waste of your taxes), clothes, food stamps, assisted housing, deliver their mostly illegitimate anchor babies and on and on! The Illegal Immigrant Criminals have bankrupted six (6) hospitals in California to date! This is a direct result of traitorous leaders with no guts including governors. Thirteen ($13,000,000,000) to eighteen billions ($18,000,000,000) of dollars totally thrown away as gifts to foreign Dictators to do as they wish with the money. (No U.S. supervision) will go a long way toward revitalizing) America .The net effect of this stupid insane giveaway is this : The countries receiving the FREE billions in so- called Foreign Aid are mostly third world dictator controlled nations totally rift with rotten government worse than the United States of America and have no obligation to use the billions to improve the lot of their people and no accounting to the United States for the actual use of the money. Again, does this speak volumes about how most of our political snots think of our own needy people? Most of them have been living off the United States of America for years- their opinion is total ignorant and jealous BS!

President Theodore Roosevelt said on August 6, 1912:

There can be no greater issue than that of conservation in this country."

Even now we have electrical power grid failures, expressways and interstate roads falling apart, flooding and destruction of natural resources, waste and garbage landfill sites ever expanding, dangerous contamination of air and water ways, collapse of education, etc., all due to exponential demands by overpopulation and lack of funds due to "giveaway" programs in the billions of dollars to Illegal Immigration Criminals. There are not enough words in the English language to express the disgust at any pinheaded idiot who declares there is enough room in America for all who want to come. Apparently these freaks have yet to reach puberty and age of reason and most certainly have diarrhea of the mouth and constipation of the brain! With destruction of towns and cities by floods as a result of population increases and clearing of millions of acres to accommodate the demand for homes, schools, ridiculous shopping malls, high rises and recreation areas comes the inevitable cost of repair and replacement which is breaking insurance companies financially, forcing them to increase premiums or dropping coverage entirely. This leads to bankruptcy of thousands of home and business owners and eventually lowers quality of life for all Americans. Infrastructure deterioration is a fact of life in every state in the union and with the present mind set of our hollow headed pseudo leaders it will continue to degrade and cripple America until

Real Americans demand and get satisfaction from these imitation political leaders. The continued influx of Illegal Criminals can only exacerbate this already critical failing condition of our infrastructure. Yet about all we hear from these miscreants is Amnesty in one form or another for the foreign invaders. What is the meaning of the word illegal? The dictionary defines it as "against the law", "forbidden by law", and "against official regulations". Could this be more explicit? Against the law means just that – how can it be interpreted to mean O.K.? Or "we forgive you" or "we give up, here is your amnesty ticket – America is yours"! This is just another example of the incompetence and gutlessness Real American citizens are faced with on a daily basis! Here we have a grown group of men elected by the people, who took a sworn oath to support the original ideas and convictions of our forefathers and the majority are acting like end stage Alzheimer victims! This is unbelievable yet it is staring us in the face that our politicians have no clue as to the effect on America if some variation of Amnesty is passed - or is it they don't care since many of them won't be around in twenty years – but perhaps you will and your kids will and their kids! There is no other decision that needs to be discussed and voted on except to bite the bullet and remove   these illegal people physically from the United States. Political Correctness is total BS for a Real American but is made to order for our elected officials.

Everybody has heard and knows the saying "sticks and stones may hurt my bones, but words will never hurt me"!   Not true with our so-called political "know-it-alls" and self titled "experts" who cringe when some loud mouth foreigner criticizes America. Their attitude should be "who cares what the rest of the stupid world thinks?" The foreign aid countries have been living off the United States of America taxpayers for years- their opinion is totally irrelevant, ignorant and jealous BS! Enough is enough!

The following describes the disgraceful and dangerous condition of America's infrastructure and certainly makes one wonder why our so-called political establishment has forsaken America and permitted this emergency to ever develop! The condition of the infrastructure in America should make every person shiver with well founded fear at the possible and probable disasters waiting to happen at any moment caused by the negligence and indifference to suffering and death of Real Americans by most of our government representatives, who in concert, agree on selling out to and supporting Illegal Immigrant Criminals with billions of taxpayer dollars instead of repairing the failing and crumbling infrastructure.

Our own Federal Government report included here substantiates the ridiculous and totally uncalled for condition of America's infrastructure! This further emphasizes the callous indifference of our political representatives to the possibilities of horrendous death tolls by failing bridges, roads, dams, railways, ancient school buildings, and inferior airport facilities.A cost estimate to repair and bring the infrastructure system up to a barely "acceptable" condition is $1.6,000,000,000,000 (one trillion six hundred billion dollars) in the next twenty years.

This will require $80,000,000,000 per year (80 Billion Dollars) per year minimum of taxpayer money!

Where is the $80 Billion dollars per year coming from? There is no possible way to provide this incredible amount of money except through one of three ways:

1. Increase the already ridiculous deficit.
2. Raise salary taxes on all Americans.
3. Increase or add excise tax on gasoline, jewelry, automobiles, entertainment, travel and accommodations, sporting goods, clothes, property, etc – practically everything needed in the course of everyday life.

So; here we are, between a rock and a hard place – thousands of American lives jeopardized by laxity, misconduct and down right ignorance in our government.

Our nation's infrastructure has fallen in disrepute and threatens the lives of thousands of American citizens.

It is not a question of if these tragedies will occur, it is a indisputable certainty unless emergency action is initiated immediately by the majority of our so-called political self- sustaining leaders. Here is the statement of one of the few elected political representatives who has the integrity to call a situation like it is and not mince words as most of our Politically Correct cowards make as a career practice. Democratic Leader Bob Rothermel, who also serves as Executive Director of the Community Advocacy Center says the following: " America's Infrastructure Is Failing Apart! He said that "according to an analysis by civil engineers concludes that our nation's transportation, water and energy systems have shown very little improvement since they were given a grade of D-plus in 2001."

The report which was released this month assessed the trends over the last two years in the condition of 12 categories of our infrastructure, that included bridges, roadways, energy, schools, airports, waste disposal, drinking water and other major threats to the quality of life for all Real Americans!

The report blamed the deteriorating infrastructure on such factors as population, Failure by the U.S. Government to control lIllegal Immigration growth, and the threat of terrorism, which caused money to be delivered to security and limited federal programs.

The other five categories of infrastructure are aviation, transit, dams, hazardous waste and navigation. The "2003 Progress Report for America's Infrastructure" showed no progress for schools which received the worst grade - D-minus in 2001 from the society. The report showed that three out of four school buildings are inadequate. The society estimates that it will cost more than $127 billion to build new classrooms and to modernize outdated schools.

Energy transmission that was rated a D-plus in 2001, and the society said the trend is declining. Investment in transmission fell by $115 million annually, to $2 billion a year in 2000 from $5 billion in 1975. The actual capacity increased by only 7,000 megawatts a year, 30 percent less than needed to keep up with the demand for power.

Rothermel said, "Our roads have never been worse, our nation is failing to even maintain the substandard conditions that currently exists. The average rush hour expanded by more than 18 minutes between 1997 and 2000." . The report also shows no improvement on our bridges. With 27.5 percent of our nations bridges being structurally deficient or obsolete in 2000. Our transportation systems have shown signs of decline, despite the increased spending over the past six years. The system cannot be maintained because it is being outpaced by the growth of ridership.

Rothermel said, "Wake up America! Everything is falling apart. In May the Bush administration proposed spending $247 billion on roads, bridges and mass transit, that is 13 percent more than the previous six-year plan. The chairman of the House Transportation and Infrastructure Committee Rep. Don Young, has proposed a $375 billion spending plan which will be paid for by indexing the gasoline tax to inflation. He noted that the report reinforced his serious concerns about the state of the U.S. infrastructure. We must do something before it's too late."

While we are exploring the major contributions to this serious threat to our lives let's not ignore the addition of 12,000,000 to 18,000,000 ILLEGAL IMMIGRANTS who have sucked up billions of dollars on top of billions of taxpayers money that should have been invested in the infrastructure. This is the epitome'of traitorous representation of REAL AMERICANS by the majority of elected politicians.

 Read these arrogant statements by Jorge Ramos – "The Latino Wave" - (Who has made a great life for himself in America and now with typical ignorance and arrogance is advocating the destruction of the very country that made him successful) and see if you still want to sit on your fanny while America is stolen by illegal criminals with cooperation of lying traitorous politicians:

 It is now your last chance to save America from trashing - it is time to crawl up the backs of and get in the face of most of our lousy traitorous so-called representatives and tell – don't ask – we demand Illegal Immigrants (Criminals) be removed from American soil and apply legally.

A new book has been published by Jorge Ramos who has been an anchorman for Noticiero Univision, the Spanish language TV network in the U.S., since 1986. The Wall Street Journal called him "Star newscaster of Hispanic TV" and "Hispanic TV's No. 1 correspondent and key to a huge voting bloc. " Naturally, the dirtbag brown nose media is swarming all over this traitorous, suggestive source of statements that America will be taken over by Mexicans . No reports have criticized this treasonous call to Mexicans to flood America and kill Gringos

Check that for Treason ignored by the menial kiss-up Media!

The research firm Hispanic Trends called Ramos "one of the most influential Latinos" in the U.S." Also a newspaper columnist, he is the winner of seven Emmy awards for journalism.

The author's opinion: A dirty low down traitor to the country that gave him all he has, and what, typically, does he give back- preaching sedition in America – nice guy, HUH?

Considering these achievements, Ramos' views and visions are well worth considering. And, as an added bonus, he presents his ideas in a mostly congenial and readable style. If it were not for the traitorous plans and suggestions presented one might give the book credible credence. However, the man is proposing in public statements to conquer another country without regard to suffering and death in the attempted criminal takeover. Ramos noticeably has come to America to preach his insane and stupid claim to America by Mexicans. What would be the answer of Ramos if asked "why do you want to destroy America, the country that gave you opportunities you would never have gotten otherwise –certainly not in Mexico." The graft and corruption in Mexico would destroy and imprison people such as Ramos. Perhaps this is the reason he is in America. It is obvious there is no place for Ramos in America except prison. Why doesn't he get out and return to Mexico if America is so terrible? He curses America and recommends her demise but he certainly likes the good life! What this mistaken person doesn't realize –like all people of his ilk – is the ignorant hordes of Mexicans will take all he has and kick him out in the street – it must be share and share alike.

> *Note: If an American citizen proposed these tactics, the FBI, CIA, and Homeland Security would haul him off to some obscure prison as a foreign agent and a threat to National Security! This is the so-called free country we live in? Think again! But Ramos is free to curse the United States and call for Mexicans to destroy us. This is confirmation of the rottenness of our system and all employees who obey like lobotomized robots in contributing to the destruction of America and their own families!*

"Beneath this **veneer of pleasantness,** however, *The Latino Wave* bears more than a passing resemblance to *Mein Kampf.* The theme throughout Ramos' book is Latino power, and he favors massive immigration from his native Mexico and other parts of Latin America to enhance that power. He is not concerned in the slightest that most of the influx is illegal. The only problem with illegal aliens, in Ramos' mind is that they are "undocumented," a problem taken care of by the second recommendation of his "Latino Agenda" (p. 219): "We must push for amnesty..." Ramos affirms (p. 213) that the Latino political power he advocates "will not forget" the politicians who opposed amnesty. A threat?

> *Note: And neither will Real American citizens!*

Does the Univision anchorman foresee assimilation by the masses of Latino immigrants? Here are his thoughts (Prologue xxi): "[Latinos], by virtue of their vast numbers ... will not completely and fully assimilate culturally. [They] are creating their own space in this country, and their particular cultural differences will continue to influence the rest of society ... [and] are forever changing the face of the United States. Latinos are shattering the proverbial concept of the melting pot."

He goes on (p. 90): "The [Latino] community has grown so much that it now seems impossible that it could ever assimilate into the Anglo-Saxon culture at large." He asks (p.187), "[Is this] an invasion? No, A cultural reconquest? It could be, at least in part ... Latinos are culturally influencing the United States in ways never seen before, and this leads us to conclude that we're becoming a Hispanic nation." (Typical BS)

Is Ramos disturbed that Latinos are not being Americanized as past waves of immigrants were? Nothing in his book suggests so. Nevertheless, he is concerned that they move beyond identities of national origin, e.g. Mexican, Cuban, etc. and see themselves as Latinos or Hispanics. This allows for a "united front" (p. 97) to enhance "political power." Ramos boasts (P. 89) that the growth of the Spanish language media is proof that "Latinos are [not] assimilating completely into U.S. society." Another perspective is that these media, which so profitably sustain Mr. Ramos, are a cause, not a consequence, of nonassimilation.

The future of the United States, as this anchorman sees it, is to offer lebensraum for the migrating masses of Latin America. In the preface he looks forward to the year 2125 when, he says, "there will be more Hispanics than non-Hispanic whites in the United States." He concludes his book by stating "the future of the United States is a Hispanic one. The Latino wave is unstoppable." Americans who object he labels "xenophobes" and "racists" (p.60). Hitler, too, had unpleasant names for people who opposed lebensraum.

Ramos is no friend of America, and certainly no friend of loyal Latino citizens and Latinos who want to be Americans. If immigrants from south of the border do not assimilate, they will replicate the Third World societies they fled-societies with a few "haves" on top and many "have nots" on the bottom. This many not be a problem for the well-heeled Mr. Ramos, but it should be a problem for all genuine Americans. Life will change for the worst!

Do you get the message now? This is War declared by Mexicans and our rotten government is totally silent!

Mass immigration will fulfill Ramos' vision. If that vision comes to pass, we cannot claim that we had no warning.

There you have it Real Americans – direct treason to the United States by calling for mass illegal immigration. (Criminal Behavior). Has there been an outcry from Senators or Congressmen condemning the direct call for killing Gringos? No, and more than likely you won't. However, what if the call had been from an American citizen to kill Mexicans who are killing more Americans than the Iraq war! There would be a hue and cry of racist, criminal, murderer, etc. from our own low down pieces of crap supposedly representing American citizens. Unbelievable treachery!

In Mexico this traitor to the country that gave him a golden opportunity, would be in prison doing hard labor for twenty years. He is showing his appreciation in the most despicable method possible – This is an example of what we are dealing with – pseudo human beings with no conscience!

Are Real Americans to stand by and watch their nation - built on the sacrifices of millions of patriots - being taken over by heathen, illegitimate aliens waltzing in with no loyalty to America and trashing this once great nation as they have Mexico? Many people are trying to spread the news that our so-called President is leading us all down the primrose path and laughing up his sleeve at our stupidity!

If our political wimpy traitors have their cowardly way this is exactly what will happen and in fact it is already happening in Arizona, California, Texas and New Mexico and the idiot politicians are running yellow belly scared – from local political crumb bums to the top levels including Governors and all the way to the top in Washington.

America is doomed if these unconscionable human reproducing machines are not transported back to their lousy Mexican "homeland" and kept out of America by whatever means necessary! America will be turned into a garbage and trash dump just like Mexico! The United States of America is now in the grip of attempted tyranny by those who have no individual integrity and honesty but ply their traitorous deeds as lies and deceit in a dastardly back stabbing mode hoping (as they would describe it), "that the stupid low life constituency won't notice until the deed is done and it's too late!"

Indeed, it **will** be too late for America if _any_ form of Amnesty is passed. The very suggestion is a lying betrayal same as the promise made by the Senate in 1986 that a one time Amnesty would be passed and NO MORE! How about 6 Times since? Does this treacherous move bolster confidence in our politicians? Lying to and cheating on voters is politicians game! They are professionals, remember?

The following article by John Vinson, President of Americans for Immigration Control, an organization attempting to bring some sanity and information into an otherwise insane effort by many U.S. Senators and Representatives to destroy America had this to say:

Reprinted by permission of John Vinson, *Editor AIC*   March 2007

"It may sound harsh to say that amnesty advocates are deceivers and liars — but it isn't harsh if it's true. Truth must be the standard because the stakes of the looming amnesty battle in Congress are so high. If we reward ten million or more illegal aliens with legal residence and the pathway to citizenship, we may well mark the beginning of the end of America, as a nation ruled by law and having a common culture.

Therefore let's examine the evidence as it reveals the character of the amnesty promoters, particularly those in Congress. You, dear readers, please be the jury.

Exhibit 1. A history of dishonesty. Pro-amnesty congressmen ask us to trust them now, but why should we? In 1986, when they passed the first amnesty, they vowed it would be a one-time only offer — and would be accompanied by strict enforcement to stop more illegal immigration. Yet hardly was the ink dry on the document before they either dragged their feet on enforcement measures, or actively sabotaged them. Then, in the following years they passed several more amnesties.

And now they have the gall to tell us that we must have another amnesty because enforcement — which they have allowed to languish — hasn't worked. Despite a few recent against hiring illegal aliens has dwindled to insignificance since its passage in 1986. And just how has amnesty worked, except to invite more illegal aliens to come and settle? Could our lawmakers explain how rewarding lawbreakers raids at worksites, overall enforcement of the law would not do the same thing again? So far, they haven't even bothered to try.

Exhibit 2. Word deception. The amnesty pushers in Congress vow and declare that their scheme really isn't an amnesty because it would set conditions for illegals to meet such as paying a fine, paying some back taxes, and learning English and American civics. They employ this semantic dodge because they know how unpopular "amnesty" is among law-abiding citizens.

To set the record straight, consider Webster's definition of amnesty: "a pardon, especially for political offenses against a government. . . . a deliberate overlooking of an offense." No suggestion here that amnesty can't have conditions. Furthermore, as pointed out by former Attorney General Edwin Meese, the 1986 amnesty — which everyone agrees was an amnesty — also had similar conditions for applicants to meet.

Exhibit 3. False promises. The very claim that we can monitor and enforce conditions for an amnesty is patently dishonest. Rampant fraud took place after passage of the '86 amnesty. So, one might inquire, what's to stop it from happening again? Certainly not the U.S. Citizenship and Immigration Services (USCIS). Last year a draft report by the Government Accountability Office (GAO) found that the agency has "a serious problem" with stopping fraud. This year, officials of the agency admitted that it could not properly administer the flood of new applications following a major amnesty. (See: *The Washington Post* 1/4/07, A03.)

Most of the pro-amnesty legislators know perfectly well that the USCIS can't deliver on the promises they make about "conditions." These promises are just sugar coating on a bitter amnesty pill to help persuade Americans to swallow it. The dishonesty and irresponsibility are breathtaking.

Exhibit 4. False alternatives. The amnesty pushers say that 12 million illegal aliens are simply too many to deport in one big roundup. Therefore, our only choice is to legalize them. Wrong. Another option is an attrition strategy, one which slowly but surely tightens enforcement, thereby encouraging many or most illegals to go back on their own.

Exhibit 5. Eyewitness testimony of deceit. Mexican diplomat Fredo Arrias-King represented his county's interests on immigration to the U.S. Congress. He revealed that a number of pro-amnesty and open border congressmen openly boasted to him that they deceive their constituents into thinking that they really trying to do something about illegal immigration. Among Republicans, he said, the aim was cheap labor; among Democrats, cheap votes.

The American people must decide and now. If your verdict is guilty, inform the offending politicians that you see through their fraud. If they refuse to shape up, sentence them to unemployment when it comes time to vote".

That this level of treason against America, by representatives duly elected and swearing an oath of office to defend the United States Of America against all enemies, Foreign and Domestic, and then corrupting themselves by completely forsaking this promise for big business racketeering purposes, and like the dumbas**s they are, expect this traitorous behavior to establish an appreciation voter base is totally incomprehensible to a normal and sane human being. This act alone re-enforces opinions of their obvious lack of credible intelligence. The character of the illegal immigrants intent on smothering America is not compatible with appreciation but is compatible with the deadly intent of assimilating their own society in America and smashing, trashing and destroying the United States of America along with the congenital idiots who made it all possible.

The fatal error that condemns this treason to failure and ignored by our traitors is the intrinsic loyalty to America and guts of the intended victims – Real Americans!

Real Americans will not stand idly by while their nation is decimated by foreigners and indifferent government pseudo officials, including our own President who has, in the opinion of millions of Genuine Americans (Not the Rich Boys) failed America miserably by approving the Illegal Immigration hordes. America is being deserted by cowardly officials who swore an oath to protect our nation!

Before America is subjugated to the ultimate indignity and collapse through internal political treason, (a multiple parallel to Benedict Arnold) there will be resistance by Real Americans and an end put to this insane cowardly betrayal of America by robber barons of big business and their political bed mates.

Arizona:

Arizona is a state in turmoil, inundated by at least a half million illegal immigrants and torn apart by ways to handle these new residents – residents? – how about illegal criminals! Homemade street signs tell day laborers to keep moving. State politicians who want to curtail illegal immigration are riding a wave of public support. And radio call-in shows -- never a bastion of civility -- debate the issue almost daily, in both English and *Español*.

Public discontent with the situation has boiled over into state policy, leading voters and lawmakers to pass some of the most hardline anti-illegal immigrant laws in the country."It brings out the worst in a lot of us," said state Rep. Steve Gallardo (D).

In May, Hispanic workers staged a one-day strike to protest the growing anti-immigrant sentiment. Hispanic leaders are calling for a nationwide boycott of Arizona, a tactic employed by civil rights groups more than a decade ago after the state refused to honor the Rev. Martin Luther King Jr. with a holiday.

That boycott cost Arizona the chance to host the 1993 Super Bowl. No guts officials and worship of money – just lay down and get trampled by ignorant invaders.

This is not a new conflict. Tensions have built for years over the influx of undocumented workers to this desert state, now the busiest illegal gateway on the Mexican border.

Federal border officials arrested nearly 500,000 people trying to enter the state between last October and July. In April, the "Minuteman

Project," a self-appointed militia, began patrolling the Arizona-Mexico border. And in mid-August, Gov. Janet Napolitano (D) took the unusual step of declaring a state of emergency. The move frees up government money to boost law enforcement along the border.

According to the Pew Hispanic Center, which like *Stateline.org* is funded by The Pew Charitable Trusts, the number of illegal immigrants in Arizona has more than quadrupled since 1996 -- from 115,000 then to about 500,000 now. By comparison, the number of illegal immigrants in the United States roughly doubled, jumping from about 5 million in 1996 to about 11 million today. The upsurge of illegal immigrants in Arizona -- on top of an economic boom that caused the state's population to increase more than 12 percent to almost 6 million since 2000 -- is severely straining prisons, schools, hospitals and law enforcement.

Some experts believe the conflict offers a glimpse into the future of American politics. Politicians in at least 11 states are pushing ballot initiative proposals similar to Arizona's ban on state services, and anti-illegal immigration measures increasingly are dividing statehouses from North Carolina to California. Arizona's turning point came last November when it became the first state since California in 1994 to adopt a ballot initiative, Proposition 200, that barred social services to illegal immigrants.

The measure, which passed with 55.6 percent of the vote despite opposition from both Democratic and Republican leaders, also makes it a crime for public employees to fail to report undocumented immigrants seeking benefits, and requires proof of citizenship to register to vote."(Illegal immigrants) can't come to America and get free stuff. It's just wrong. You've got to take their benefits away," said Rep. Russell Pearce (R), who led the Prop 200 drive. Unlike California's initiative, Arizona's Prop 200 has held up in court. In early August, a federal appeals court rejected a lawsuit aimed at overturning it. Further legal action is expected.

Prop 200 has done little to change the lives of illegal immigrants, who cannot legally vote anyway and were eligible only for limited benefits. But its passage galvanized conservative state lawmakers to introduce additional punitive measures during this year's session of the Legislature. Several measures passed, were signed into law by the governor and went into effect Aug. 12. Arizona police officers, as well as federal border patrol officers, now can arrest people suspected of smuggling illegal immigrants into the United States. They also can seize vehicles driven by illegal immigrants that are involved in an accident. State judges can lengthen a felony sentence if the person convicted has violated federal immigration law, and city and county officials are barred from spending on migrant work centers, which illegal immigrants often use to find employment. Governor Napolitano vetoed proposals to designate English as the official state language and build a prison in Mexico for illegal immigrants.

In 2006, Arizona voters will consider changing the state Constitution to deny bail to illegal immigrants arrested for serious crimes. GOP lawmakers are considering going around Napolitano to revive the English-only proposal and put it on the ballot, too, as well as another initiative that would give local police the power to arrest illegal immigrants.

Carlos Morales, who illegally immigrated from Mexico about 18 months ago, said in an interview at a work center in northern Phoenix that the law that ends funding to work centers is typical of politics in the aftermath of Prop 200. "After Proposition 200, it seems everything is against the migrant. It's racist. Everything seems to be blamed on the migrant," Morales said in Spanish through a translator. Well, they deserve it for attempting to trash America and being a criminal! Although undocumented workers help provide labor for Arizona's booming construction business, they also impose costs. Jim Dickson, who runs a hospital five miles from the Mexican border, says emergency room care for illegal immigrants has risen from $30,000 to more than $350,000 in only four years. "We're in a war down here to preserve the health system," said Dickson.

Law enforcement officials and lawmakers such as Pearce also contend that crime follows illegal immigrants across the border. The state prison system spent $77 million last year detaining more than 4,000 illegal immigrants.

Compounding the tension, Arizona residents can't even agree on what to call those who illegally cross the border; the gamut runs from the conservative label "illegal aliens" to the liberal "undocumented workers." How abut "Criminals"? To some, much of the conflict is ethnic: Hispanics in 2003 comprised over 27 percent of Arizona's population. Of the 449,000 new residents added between 2000 and 2003, more than 53 percent were Hispanic. Census figures do not differentiate between legal and illegal residents.

State Sen. Karen Johnson (R) sees a cultural struggle, too. "The culture of the United States is being destroyed," she said. **"The illegals don't want to be a part of American** culture. **They want to bring their Mexican-Hispanic culture here."** As the number of Hispanics living in the state has grown, so has the number of Hispanic state legislators, who now hold 14 of the 90 seats in the Statehouse. Stupidity never ceases. Rodolfo Espino of Arizona State University, who specializes in political behavior and minority politics, said this increased political power may explain some of the current anti-immigration sentiment in Arizona. The white establishment is in danger of losing control, he said. The United States was built by "Yankees" and whatever it takes, will remain a "Yankee" nation – screw the Illegal Immigrants –they had better hit the road back to the lousy country they came from and come back legally! But the sentiment driving Arizona's backlash can be found even within the Hispanic community. Prop 200 exit polls showed that 47 percent of Hispanics who voted supported the measure. Rita Montanez, a mother of three who lives in Mesa, Ariz., worries about the effects of illegal immigration on her ability to get health care. "I'm Mexican-American, and I just believe we are overstretched because of all the immigration," Montanez said. She added that "closing the border" might be the only solution to the problem.

Taking a real life look down the road, Texas, California, New Mexico and Arizona are apparently controlled by Mexican Illegal Criminals now with cowardly officials afraid to arrest and deport them. Where are the Governors and police officials - are they being told to layoff by George Bush? Recent events have demonstrated the cowardice of mayors and city councils in many cities where demonstrations by these half-witted uneducated idiot Illegal Criminals have sent the city officials scurrying for cover like frightened rats – is this no guts or Political pressure from certain elements of our weak government?

How long since a Senator, Congressman or President was impeached? Bill Clinton escaped justice due to "party loyalty above all" mentalities. This is typical American politics and lends credence to America being the most corrupt nation on the face of the earth! There are quite a few (actually 62 traitors) who are seriously considering placing America in jeopardy of total extinction when they violate their sworn oath by castrating America with a rotten, low down, sneaking, deceitful and traitorous Amnesty vote for self acclaimed Mexican "Gringo" killers! If this happens, justice will be served at the impeachment hearings and convictions of these traitors. Voting social security and amnesty for Illegal Immigrant is a crime against America and deserves severe punishment! It is incomprehensible these imbeciles would vote to sentence their own families – wives, children and their children – to a life of hell on earth orchestrated by Mexican dirtbags – a society of crass ignorant fools cloning America in the image of lousy Mexico! It is typical of the insolence, stupidity, total arrogance and lying indifferent greed that has personified most of our political figures in recent years. Our predicament demands relief from such monsters of deception, treason and betrayal as is so inherent and characteristic of our ELECTED so-called representatives now intending to flood America with their dumb-a.. concept of cheap labor for Big Business Racketeers, Cheap Votes for Democrats. This is evidence of Alzheimer infection and the only cure is to open the door and boot the disease out. America is being betrayed by both lying parties and in the fatal murderous process of killing America are showing their true color (Yellow) and contempt for Real Americans. Betrayal of America is not acceptable as those responsible will learn the hard way! American politics – both parties - is rotten to the core except for a tiny minority who are to be praised for their efforts against the agents of America's destruction. – but we must hear from them loud and clear! There must be a house cleaning of gigantic proportions to cleanse America of the stench and smell of political decay and rottenness permeating our political system – from top to bottom. Real and Genuine Americans – all colors, will not lay down and be trampled on, robbed of their heritage, their land, murdered and raped by gangs, just to satisfy the treasonous stupid, political expediency of the majority of congenital idiots calling themselves representatives of Real Americans. The laws of physics state for every action there is a equal reaction. In America our rotting political thieves should understand the truth of this postulate - that there will most certainly be a direct reaction to their action – perhaps totally unexpected in nature and proportion.

One of the most unfathomable anti-American acts of treachery is the mental aberrations of many of the rich. The majority of these are recipients of inherited fortunes – and could not pour pee out of a boot with directions on the heel. However, this screwed up mentality becomes obsessed with notions of superiority. The next step to them is obvious: anything goes, money will insure my future: open the borders; remember, Mr. George Bush has not been forthcoming and honest with Americans – rather he has sidestepped with actual dishonesty, certainly not befitting his position as chief executive and trusted by Real Americans. It is the opinion now, as one looks back at his career as Governor of Texas, that he is the one person mostly responsible for the over 12 Million Mexicans in America! How's that for trustworthiness? To many thousands of Real Americans his Open Border policy has been as obvious as has his misleading remarks on illegal criminal immigration which he has not the slightest intention of stopping! There are many astute interpreters of world affairs who are concerned this is part of the planned takeover of America and precursor of One World Order – all envisioned by the "Rich Elite" planners. Now, with the support of many treasonous members of the Senate and Congress, who don't know their A.. from a hole in the ground, this planned destruction of America's sovereignty is moving right along. While the people are asleep and distracted by a family grudge war. A personification of this is the North American Union project now underway to join Mexico, the United States and Canada as one giant society under one trilateral flag thus destroying the sovereignty of America. There will be no more America per se! Looking back at what has transpired with the rotten effort to swamp America with Mexicans and thus continue the watering down of American society, many questions have been raised as to why the

Iraq travesty just happened to be coincidental with the flooding of America by Illegal Immigrants. Could the war be a planned distraction?

Counting on the total chaos and confusion reigning in America as the nation is flooded with millions more Mexicans, the One World Order traitors will be able to devise control mechanisms unnoticed by the betrayed Americans. The millions of Mexicans who think they are so clever are nothing but pawns in the "Elite's" game of human chess.

Thomas Jefferson said:

"Experience hath shewn, that even under the best forms of government those entrusted perverted it into tyranny!"

This is exactly the program under way in America and the lazy, indifferent "Let the Good Times Roll" crowd had better wake up before becoming prisoners of tyranny from which there is no escaping! Your own brothers and sons in the military will be ordered to shoot you like mad dogs if any resistance is attempted, but realize also, this is not the case with rioting Mexicans who rape, murder and rob with impunity – can the reader understand the plan now and who is behind it from top to bottom in our government? Talk to Arnold Schwarzenegger and get his take on a betrayed America!

There will be no other opportunity to save America from the traitors in our midst.

The United States Senate has 100 Members and the House of Representatives has 435 members and most of these (except a very few patriots) have a very dim view of the intelligence of voters. The general opinion of most Real Americans polled is that the U.S. Senate is by far the most saturated and disgraced by those who are intending, because of cowardice and personal rottenness, to betray America through a treasonous vote by 62 Senators to vote for Amnesty. The sad and at the same time angering abandonment of the people's wishes by these liars is the stark and rude awakening fact that we, the people, have been snookered by the Mr. Jekyll and Mr. Hyde personalities elected by trusting voters! One wonders what would be the response if en masse, these so-called lousy representatives of the people were asked: "are you proud of betraying the Real Americans who placed total faith in you to respond to their wishes?" A personal poll of 100 Real Americans were asked to compare the list of Senators below who voted for Amnesty to Benedict Arnold. Ninety - seven percent replied "The same". "Just as Bad", "worse, because there are so many"

Now is the time to get MAD AS HELL and let these traitors among us feel the venom of your bite! Remember the Merriam- Webster definition of Traitor?:

One who betrays another's trust or is false to an obligation or duty.

VOTING FOR AMNESTY FOR CRIMINALS QUALIFIES AS A PERFECT MATCH TO THE DEFINITION OF **TRAITOR. (This also qualifies for impeachment!).**

Let's take a moment to repeat the oath of office for Senators of the United States of America and see how their performance matches their sworn statement:

<u>**Oath required by the Constitution and by Law to be taken by Government officials when taking office:**</u>

I,_A,B_, do solemnly swear or (affirm) that I will support and defend the Constitution of the United States against all enemies, foreign and domestic, that I will bear true faith and allegiance to the same, that I take this obligation freely, without any mental reservation or purpose of evasion; and that I will well and faithfully discharge the office of which I am about to enter.

So Help Me God! _

Even the sloppiest and most liberal interpretation of the oath above cannot help but point out with dramatic certainty the direct intentional betrayal of their sworn oath of office. There is no evading the truth of what these people have committed against their own nation. They swore on the bible to defend America against all enemies foreign and domestic but have crawled under their respective desks to hide from the truth!

Read the following to confirm he treachery facing the American people and perpetrated by none other than trusted political representatives and George Bush is on top of the disgusting heap!

ARTICLE IV, SECTION 4 OF THE U.S. CONSTITUTION

"The United States shall guarantee to every State in this Union a Republican Form of Government, and shall protect each of them against invasion; and on Application of the Legislature, or of the Executive (when the Legislature cannot be convened) against domestic Violence."

You see directly before your eyes the Federal Government guarantee required by the Constitution to states and their citizens of protection from invasion. There is no other true word or interpretation for the smothering hordes from Mexico except Invaders.

Therefore, it is an indefensible crime and betrayal of American state sovereignty to permit or allow millions of Illegal Immigrants (Criminals by definition) to invade the United States of America.

In consideration of the above, United States citizens demand true allegiance to the Constitution of the United States of America as sworn to by all officials of the United States Government:The United States Senate and House of Representatives or immediate resignation in preference to the dishonor of impeachment!

There can be no reconcilable or equitable solution to the murderous intentions of the Mexican hordes except to load them all up and haul them back to Mexico – by force if necessary. Damn the cost! Americans are fed up with the Republicans who are in the pockets of Big Business Racketeers and the Democrats who will sell their souls and betray America for votes.

It is all so stupid and points out the obvious: The majority of those attempting to sell America down the river don't know their As… from a hole in the ground which is confirmed by their crimes against the American people!

Two Faced Nancy Pelosi
Speaker of the House

THERE IS COMING TO PUBLIC attention very disquieting news about Speaker of the House Nancy Pelosi and her continuing insane push to have her way in the certain destruction of America At the same time she is ranting and raving about the qualities lacking in the Republican Party, she is at the same time being a traitor to Real Americans and going to bed with Illegal Aliens. Defining traitor from the dictionary we read: "One who betrays a trust, his country, friends, an oath or promise." There is no lower personality trait than to betray a trust and a sworn oath.

What is sorely needed in America is a political house cleaning of traitors and despots by the small minority of Real Americans like Representative Tom Tancredo R- CO, Representative Duncan R-CA , Representative Dana Rohrabacher R-CA and Representative Duncan Hunter, R-CA who would be performing a inestimable service to America by bring up charges of treason and disgrace the American traitors in our midst. Admittedly, after all the heads have rolled, there will not be many left standing – but so be it for the survival of America. An appeal to Real Americans will bring all the backup required to send these traitors into oblivion as they are attempting to do America!

It has come to light that Nancy Pelosi - you know -   the worst human being who could ever have been selected as Speaker of the House – has millions of dollars of non-union vineyards in Napa Valley. As would be expected of a person of her caliber, she of course uses foreign labor – what kind you ask? Illegal Immigrants of course and naturally is doing everything she can to help open the floodgates to more illegal immigration. This is against the law – what does the word ILLEGAL mean? And she wants the American taxpayers to pay their way. Just who in Hell does she think she is? And she voted in favor of rewarding illegal aliens from Mexico with Social Security benefits – a treasonous act against America most Americans would condemn. This traitor has betrayed America for profit and nothing could be more disgusting than to watch her strutting around as though she should have red carpet rolled out for her.

So, using Illegal Immigrants - breaking the law – and further sinking into depths of degradation and treason against Real Americans – apparently worship of money is number one priority with this traitor. Nancy Pelosi has: led the Democratic opposition to any effective border controls or documentation requirements. She opposed the Secure Fence Act of 2006, signed into law by President Bush, and voted against final passage of a border security and enforcement bill in 2005 which required that all businesses must use an electronic system to check if all new hires have the legal right to work in this country. She voted against a bill to bar drivers' licenses for illegal aliens in 2005. This year she opposed legislation requiring presentation of a legitimate government-issued photo ID to prove eligibility to vote, claiming that "there is little evidence anywhere in the country of a significant problem with non-citizen voters." Liar –Liar –your A** should be on fire. For example, an accused terrorist by the name of Nuradin Abdi was just recently reported to have illegally registered to vote at the Ohio Bureau of Motor Vehicles. Nuradin Abdi was indicted earlier this year as part of a conspiracy to blow up the Columbus Mall.

How many other terrorist suspects may have slipped through the system because Leftists like Pelosi oppose any meaningful screens? Instead she continues to advocate our recognition of the flimsy, non-validated ID card that the Mexican consulates provide to illegal aliens before they cross over our border, called the "matricula consular", which gives them phony documentation to set up bank accounts, apply for jobs, obtain social benefits, board airplanes, identify themselves to police, enter buildings that require IDs, obtain drivers' licenses and then perhaps use those drivers' licenses to try to illegally register to vote in our elections.

This traitor believes believes in giving sanctuary to illegal aliens – Mexicans or Terrorists. She opposed legislation to deny federal homeland security funding to state and local governments who refuse to share information they learn about an individual's immigration status with Federal immigration authorities. Pelosi is from San Francisco is one of the sanctuary cities she voted to protect for the benefit of illegal aliens. Pelosi even voted against deporting terrorists, afraid the bill would somehow include Illegal Immigrants. Democrats aren't just hypocrites, in addition they are working actively to subvert our legislative system to their own ends. Their only goal is votes, votes and more votes, no matter where they come from, no matter if they're cast legally, no matter whether the person casting them is dead, alive, a citizen or an illegal alien." Low down and dirty. This is American traitors working against America and should be impeached.

Pelosi regards anyone opposing her wide open employment of illegals a threat to her pro-illegal alien agenda. More illegal aliens mean more votes for the Democrats and more grape-pickers for Napa Valley vineyards like hers. So she even voted against a measure that would have cut off the use of U.S. taxpayers' funds to tip off illegal aliens as to where the Minutemen citizen patrols may be located! She obviously wants to see any kind of spotlight on her illegal activities short circuited like her traitorous brain. She can count on the liberal press to distort the real facts no matter how many lies have to be told.

To show the depths of brainwashing college students are swallowing hook line and sinker –fed this unholy diet by insane professors (who by the way will be among the first to be stomped in the ground by hordes of heathens rampaging in America) Fox News played a clip of the disgraceful performance by idiot students attacking the stage where Jim Gilchrist was just beginning a speech in early October. He was prevented from finishing his speech at the "Minutemen Forum" sponsored by the Columbia College Republicans. Gilchrist had spoken for just a few minutes and managed to utter the words "I love the First Amendment" when a group of radical moron scumbag protestors took the stage and interrupted him, displaying a big banner saying "There are no illegals." More idiot protestors then stormed the stage. Chaos erupted and the audience members who had come to hear Gilchrist speak never got the chance, which was precisely the protestors' objective. As reported online by the staff of Columbia's undergraduate newspaper, "a mosh pit of triumphal students and community members danced and chanted outside, "Asian, Black, Brown and White, we smashed the Minutemen tonight!" Real intelligent kids, HUH? Mom and Dad should yank their tails home and put 'em to work sacking groceries!

Where were Columbia College security people and where was the President and why was not punishment for these pieces of crap students made public. (Probably there was none!) Political Correctness and no guts by yellow officials. American Colleges and Universities are staffed with communists and socialist moron professors –professional career students who have never worked a day in their life, are afraid to face the outside world, yet mouth off from the security blanket of their college office and infiltrate the oatmeal brains of weak minded students with total babble.

If the President of Columbia College had an ounce of integrity these crummy pieces of crap students would have been kicked out of school permanently, This type of disgraceful activity is absolutely uncalled for and represents contempt for anything American. Mealy mouth excuses is the order of business for school officials and represents the decadent mindset prevalent in our education facilities today. A universal expression applies to virtually all school officials: Diarrhea of the Mouth and Constipation of the Brain!

Such Leftists think that migration in a borderless world is a basic human right. They want no barriers, no guards, and no proof of lawful residency. They certainly do not want the Minutemen watching the border and reporting illegal entry to the authorities.

So, with this type of sick minds saturating learning institutions including not only pea brain students but professors and staff, is it any wonder at the decadent decaying status of our learning institutions in America?

These are the type of yellow spine cowards who will kiss the boots of the savage invaders and get the hell beat out of 'em for their trouble. Brave when they gang attack speakers, cowards when they are confronted! There is only the usual cover up stupidity indicating a total lack of "college" brains when we hear complaints of discrimination and violations of so – called rights of Illegal Immigrants. Possibly, most of the far left students at these communist/socialist hideouts are too dumb to write a clear description and meaning of the word ILLEGAL! Immigrants who follow our rules are welcome here. Those who do not abide by our laws have no right to be here. A person who breaks into your house without your permission does not deserve room, board and a job as a reward, even if the intruder may be much poorer than you. He has broken the law and deserves to be punished for what he has done. Our country's boundaries and rules for entry and residency similarly define who is permitted to be here and how we choose to protect ourselves. We are a land of immigrants, but we are also a land of laws with certain core values. The trash entering our country illegally demand we hand over our land, our treasures, our traditions and threaten to kill us if we do not! Where is our pseudo president George Bush (He does not deserve the respect of the office he has disgraced) while we are being attacked, our nation impugned and properties destroyed? Mexico's foreign Secretary wants to drag us before the United Nations for intending to build a fence on our side of the border with our money to keep out aliens who seek to enter our country illegally and George Bush will probably agree. They will probably get a sympathetic ear as some UN bureaucrats believe there should be no such thing as "illegal" immigrants in the first place. For the first time in our history, Americans are being asked to cede the right to decide how we define ourselves as a nation and protect our own borders to a globalist governance body. Will Pelosi lead her liberal brainless traitor loyalists as House Speaker to support the UN against America's right to control its own borders? Do we really want to risk finding out? No, write this un-American and tell her thousands of voters consider her a traitor. Impeachment for treason will be next if she doesn't resign! It is unbelievable Republicans have not demanded she step down as unfit and certainly unqualified for office. On the other side of the coin are traitors from the Republican camp. The few good Americans we do have in the house need to carry this message to the American people and demand Nancy Pelosi's ouster as a threat to the nation!

Illegal aliens are killing more Americans than the Iraq war, says a new report from Family Security Matters that estimates some 2,158 murders are committed every year by illegal aliens in the U.S.

Ninety-five percent of warrants for murder in Los Angeles, Calif. are for illegal aliens.

Eighty-three percent of warrants for murder in Phoenix, Ariz. are for illegal aliens.

The Siesta and Fiesta is a built-in national trait of Mexico and the country can wait until the Siesta and Fiesta is over. No, the lazy and incompetent would rather complain of losing a war they started and lost and how unfair it was. Nobody complained when the United States gave them a check for $15 Million dollars gratis and later $10 Million for a railroad right of way which today would equate to $1Billion. The money was gobbled up by corruption and the citizens never realized one peso of benefit. If every Mexican in Mexico was given $500,000 cash, today, in three months it would be gone, gambling, new automobiles, women wine and song, sex, whatever – it would be in many other pockets and he would still be broke. This is the Mexican lifestyle and trashing America will be a natural Mexican pastime just as in Mexico! The lie by Mexican discontents and traitors is a deliberate plan to foment unrest among ignorant citizens and also play on emotions of many stupid BB brain Americans.- especially those tunnel vision yo-yo brain professor types in our Universities!

What you would see is a country that is an exact replica of present day Mexico. Garbage and trash, no people with industry and inquisitive minds to bring about better conditions and prosperity only a lazy shiftless mode of existence, siesta, fiesta and drugs. A national personality dedicated to sucking up products of other nations while contributing nothing but problems and more illegitimate kids. Now, this national trait has been approved by the majority of scumbag United States Politicians as deserving of everything America has to offer – free of charge. It's past time for a thorough house cleaning in the United States Government while we still have a chance to save our country from destruction by approved hordes of illegal invaders! The question again: What is it about the meaning of ILLEGAL that the majority of our dirtbag politicians in America do not seem to be able to understand? Perhaps it's because 95% of politicians are lawyers?

When Americans started settling in Texas and in 1836 became the majority, they decided to secede and join the American Union – they had nothing in common with Mexicans so why not. However this was not acceptable to Mexico and the conflict began to fester.

For those who may have a tendency to believe the lies and exaggerations of dumb bleeding hearts and certain traitorous politicians, in addition to the outlaw Mexican gangs, the true account of the Mexican-American war is presented below. The threats and stinking lies thrown about by scurrilous treasonous Mexican organizations are total crap and designed to incite their dumb ignorant followers:

When Mexico gained independence from the Spanish Empire in the Mexican War of Independence, it inherited ownership of the provinces of Alta California, Nuevo Mexico, Colorado, Utah, the Arizona Territories and Texas, from Spain. These territories are all now States within the borders of the United States of America. The new Mexican government, weakened and virtually bankrupt from the Mexican War of Independence, found it difficult to govern its northern territories, which in any case were up to two thousand miles from the capital of Mexico City.

In the mid-1830s, the government of Mexico, under General Santa Anna, attempted to centralize power. However, several Mexican states rebelled against his government, including Texas (then a department of the state of Coahuila y Tejas), San Luis Potosí, Querétaro, Durango, Guanajuato, Michoacán, Yucatán, Jalisco and [[Zacatecas] under Santa Anna. Technically, the legal grievance was abolition of the federalist Constitution of 1824 in favor of a centralist government under Santa Anna. The violent insurgency started in Texas and, to this day is known as the Texas Revolution.

In the successful 1836 Texas Revolution, Texas won its independence after defeating Santa Anna and the Mexican army. General Santa Anna was taken captive by the Texas militia and only released after he promised to recognize the sovereignty of the Republic of Texas. When Santa Anna returned to Mexico however, the government refused to recognize the loss or independence of the Republic of Texas because, the Mexicans said, Santa Anna was not a representative of Mexico and that he signed away Texas under duress. Mexico declared its intention to recapture what it considered a breakaway province.

In the decade after 1836, Texas consolidated its position as an independent republic by establishing diplomatic ties with Great Britain, France, and the United States. Most Texans were in favor of annexation by the United States, but Andrew Jackson rejected it. Texas was admitted to the union in 1845, when it became the 28th state. The Mexican government had long warned that annexation meant war with the United States. Britain and France, which recognized the independence of Texas, repeatedly tried to dissuade Mexico from declaring war against a much more powerful neighbor. British efforts to mediate were fruitless in part because additional political disputes (particularly the Oregon boundary dispute) arose between Britain and the United States.

In 1845, U.S. President James K. Polk, sent diplomat John Slidell to Mexico City in an attempt to purchase Mexico's California and New Mexico territories. U.S. expansionists wanted California to thwart British ambitions in the area and to have a Pacific port. Polk authorized Slidell to forgive the $4.5 million owed to U.S. citizens from the Mexican War of Independence and pay another $25 to $30 million in exchange for the two territories.

However, Mexico was not inclined nor in a position to negotiate. In 1846 alone, the presidency changed hands four times, the war ministry six times, and the finance ministry sixteen times. [1] According to historian Miguel Soto, Mexican public opinion and Mexican political factions and leaders felt Mexico's honor would be diminished by selling any territory. Mexicans opposing open conflict with the United States, including President José Joaquín de Herrera, were viewed as traitors. When de Herrera considered receiving Slidell in order to peacefully negotiate the problem of Texas annexation, he was accused of treason and deposed.

Military opponents of President José Joaquín de Herrera considered Slidell's presence in Mexico City an insult. After a more nationalistic government under General Mariano Paredes y Arrillaga came to power, the new government publicly reaffirmed Mexico's claim to Texas, and Slidell left in a temper, convinced that Mexico should be "chastized."

 By then, Polk had received word of the Thornton Affair and added this to the rejection of Slidell as the casus belli. A message to Congress on May 11, 1846, stated that Mexico had "invaded our territory and shed American blood upon the American soil." A joint session of Congress approved the declaration of war, mostly because southern Democrats strongly supported the war. 67 Whigs voted against it on a key slavery amendment, but on the final passage only 14 Whigs voted no, including Representatives Abraham Lincoln and John Quincy Adams. The United States declared war on Mexico on May 13, 1846, and Mexico officially declared war on July 7 (sometimes the manifest from President Paredes on May 23 is construed as the declaration of war, but only the Mexican congress had that power).

Whigs in both the North and the South generally opposed the war, while most Democrats supported it. Whig Congressman Abraham Lincoln contested the causes for the war, and demanded to know the exact spot on which Thornton had been attacked and U.S. blood had been shed. He was quoted as saying "Show me the spot." Whig leader Robert Toombs of Georgia declared:

"This war is a nondescript.... We charge the President with usurping the war-making power... with seizing a country... which had been for centuries, and was then in the possession of the Mexicans.... Let us put a check upon this lust of dominion. We had territory enough, Heaven knew."

Northern abolitionists attacked the war as an attempt by slave-owners — frequently referred to as "the Slave Power" — to expand the grip of slavery and thus assure their continued influence in the federal government. Acting on his convictions, Henry David Thoreau was jailed for his refusal to pay taxes to support the war, and penned his famous essay, Civil Disobedience.

Former President John Quincy Adams also expressed his belief that the war was fundamentally an effort to expand slavery. In response to such concerns, Democratic Congressman David Wilmot introduced the Wilmot Proviso, which aimed to prohibit slavery in any new territory acquired from Mexico. Wilmot's proposal did not pass Congress, but it spurred further hostility between the factions.

After the declaration of war, U.S. forces invaded Mexican territory on two main fronts. The U.S. war department sent a cavalry force under Stephen W. Kearny to invade western Mexico from Fort Leavenworth, reinforced by a Pacific fleet under John D. Sloat. This was done primarily because of concerns that Britain might also attempt to occupy the area. Two more forces, one under John E. Wool and the other under Taylor, were ordered to occupy Mexico as far south as the city of Monterrey.

When the US declared war against Mexico, on May 13, 1846, it took almost two months (mid-July 1846) for definite word of war to get to California. U.S. consul Thomas O. Larkin, stationed in Monterey, on hearing rumors of war tried to keep peace between the U.S. and the small Mexican military garrison commanded by José Castro. U.S. Army captain John C. Frémont with about 60 well-armed men had entered California in December 1845 and was making a slow march to Oregon when they received word that war between Mexico and the U.S. was imminent.]

On June 15, 1846, some 30 settlers, mostly U.S. citizens, staged a revolt and seized the small Mexican garrison in Sonoma. They raised the "Bear Flag" of the California Republic over Sonoma. It lasted one week until the U.S. Army, led by Fremont, took over on June 23. The California state flag today is based on this original Bear Flag, and still contains the words "California Republic."

Commodore John Drake Sloat, on hearing of imminent war and the revolt in Sonoma, ordered his naval forces to occupy Yerba Buena (present San Francisco) on July 7 and raise the American flag. On July 15, Sloat transferred his command to Commodore Robert F. Stockton, a much more aggressive leader, who put Frémont's forces under his orders. On July 19, Frémont's "California Battalion" swelled to about 160 additional men from newly arrived settlers near Sacramento, and he entered Monterey in a joint operation with some of Stockton's sailors and marines. The word had been received — the war was official. The U.S. forces easily took over the north of California; within days they controlled San Francisco, Sonoma, and Sutter's Fort in Sacramento.

In Northern California, Mexican General José Castro and Governor Pío Pico fled to Mexico . When Stockton's forces, sailing south to San Diego, stopped in San Pedro, he dispatched 50 US Marines, and entered Los Angeles unresisted on August 13, 1846, known as the Siege of Los Angeles, the nearly bloodless conquest of California seemed complete. Stockton, however, left too small a force in Los Angeles, and the Californios, acting on their own and without help from Mexico, led by José Mariá Flores , forced the American garrison to retreat in late September. More than 300 reinforcements sent by Stockton, led by U.S. Navy Captain William Mervine, were repulsed in the Battle of Dominguez Rancho, October 7 through October 9, 1846, near San Pedro, where 14 U.S. Marines were killed. The rancho vaqueros, banned together to defend their land, fighting as Californio Lancers, became a force to deal with the Americans had not planned on. Meanwhile, General Stephen W. Kearny, with a squadron of 139 dragoons, finally reached California after a grueling march across New Mexico, Arizona and the Sonora desert, on December 6, 1846, and was defeated by the Californio Lancers at the Battle of San Pasqual near San Diego, California, where 22 of Kearny's troops were killed.

Stockton rescued Kearny's retreating forces and later, with their re-supplied, combined force, marched north from San Diego, entering the Los Angeles area on January 8, 1847, linking up with Frémont's men. With U.S. forces totaling 660 soldiers and marines, they fought and defeated the 160 man Californio force in the decisive Battle of Rio San Gabriel, and the next day, January 9, 1847, they fought the

Battle of La Mesa. On January 12, 1847, the last significant body of Californios surrendered to U.S. forces. That marked the end of the War in California. On January 13, 1847, the Treaty of Cahuenga was signed.

On January 28, 1847, U.S. Army Lieutenant William Tecumseh Sherman and his army unit arrived in Monterey, California as U.S. forces in the pipeline continued to stream into California. On March 15, 1847, Col. Jonathan D. Stevenson's Seventh Regiment of New York Volunteers of about 900 men started arriving in California. All of these men were in place when word went out that gold was discovered in California, January 1848.

The defeats at Palo Alto and Resaca de la Palma caused political turmoil in Mexico, turmoil which Antonio López de Santa Anna used to revive his political career and return from self-imposed exile in Cuba. He promised the U.S. troops that if allowed to pass through their blockade, he would negotiate a peaceful conclusion to the war and sell the New Mexico and California territories to the United States. Once he arrived in Mexico, however, he reneged and offered his military skills to the Mexican government. After he had been appointed general he reneged again and seized the presidency.

2,300 U.S. troops led by Taylor crossed the Rio Grande (Rio Bravo) after some initial difficulties in obtaining river transport. He occupied the city of Matamoros, then Camargo (where while waiting the soldiery suffered the first of many problems with disease) and then proceeded south and besieged the city of Monterrey. This Battle of Monterrey was a hard fought battle during which both sides suffered serious losses. The American light artillery was ineffective against the stone fortifications of the city. The Mexican forces were under General Pedro de Ampudia. A U.S. infantry division and the Texas Rangers captured four hills to the west of the town and with them heavy cannon. That lent the U.S. soldiers the strength to storm the city from the west and east. Once in the city, U.S. soldiers fought house to house: each was cleared by throwing lighted shells, which worked like grenades. Eventually, these actions drove and trapped Ampudia's men into the city's central plaza, where howitzer shelling forced Ampudia to negotiate. Taylor agreed to allow the Mexican Army to evacuate and to an 8-week armistice in return for the surrender of the city. Under pressure from Washington, Taylor broke the armistice and occupied the city of Saltillo, southwest of Monterrey. Santa Anna blamed the loss of Monterrey and Saltillo on Ampudia and demoted him to command a small artillery battalion.

On February 22, 1847, Santa Anna personally marched north to fight Taylor with 20,000 men. Taylor, with 4,600 men, had entrenched at a mountain pass called Buena Vista. Santa Anna suffered desertions on the way north and arrived with 15,000 men in a tired state. He demanded and was refused surrender of the U.S. army; he attacked the next morning. Santa Anna flanked the U.S. positions by sending his cavalry and some of his infantry up the steep terrain that made up one side of the pass, while a division of infantry attacked frontally along the road leading to Buena Vista. Furious fighting ensued during which the U.S. troops were almost routed, but were saved by artillery fire against a Mexican advance at close range by Captain Braxton Bragg, and a charge by the mounted Mississippi Riflemen under Jefferson Davis. Having suffered discouraging losses, Santa Anna withdrew that night, leaving Taylor in control of Northern Mexico. Polk distrusted Taylor, whom he felt had shown incompetence in the Battle of Monterrey by agreeing to the armistice, and may have considered him a political rival for the White House. Taylor later used the Battle of Buena Vista as the centerpiece of his successful 1848 presidential campaign.

Rather than reinforce Taylor's army for a continued advance, President Polk sent a second army under General Winfield Scott, which was transported to the port of Veracruz by sea, to begin an invasion of the Mexican heartland. Scott performed the first major amphibious landing in the history of the United States in preparation for the Siege of Veracruz. A group of 12,000 volunteer and regular soldiers successfully offloaded supplies, weapons and horses near the walled city. Included in the invading force were Robert E. Lee, George Meade, Ulysses S. Grant, and Thomas "Stonewall" Jackson. The city was defended by Mexican General Juan Morales with 3,400 men.

Mortars and naval guns under Commodore Matthew C. Perry were used to reduce the city walls and harass defenders. The city replied as best it could with its own artillery. The effect of the extended barrage destroyed the will of the Mexican side to fight against a numerically superior force, and they surrendered the city after 12 days under siege. U.S. troops suffered 80 casualties, while the Mexican side had around 180 killed and wounded, about half of whom were civilian. During the siege, the U.S. side began to fall victim to yellow fever.

Scott then marched westward toward Mexico City with 8,500 healthy troops, while Santa Anna set up a defensive position in a canyon around the main road at the halfway mark to Mexico City, near the hamlet of Cerro Gordo. Santa Anna had entrenched with 12,000 troops and artillery that were trained on the road, along which he expected Scott to appear. However, Scott had sent 2,600 mounted dragoons ahead, and the Mexican artillery prematurely fired on them and revealed their positions. Instead of taking the main road, Scott's troops trekked through the rough terrain to the north, setting up his artillery on the high ground and quietly flanking the Mexicans. Although by then aware of the positions of U.S. troops, Santa Anna and his troops were unprepared for the onslaught that followed. The Mexican army was routed. The U.S. army suffered 400 casualties, while the Mexicans suffered over 1,000 casualties and 3,000 were taken prisoner.

In May, Scott pushed on to Puebla, the second largest city in Mexico. Because of the citizens' hostility to Santa Anna, the city capitulated without resistance on May 1. Mexico City was laid open in the Battle of Chapultepec and subsequently occupied.

Winfield Scott became an American national hero after his victories in the Mexican War, and later became military governor of occupied Mexico City.

The novel, Gone For Soldiers, by Jeff Shaara, explains a great deal of General Scott's campaign, from the point of view of three characters. These characters were Colonel Robert E. Lee, General Winfield Scott, and Mexican Dictator Antonio López de Santa Anna.

The Treaty of Guadalupe Hidalgo, signed on February 2, 1848 by American diplomat Nicholas Trist, ended the war and gave the U.S undisputed control of Texas, established the U.S.-Mexican border of the Rio Grande River, and ceded to the United States California, Nevada, Utah, and parts of Colorado, Arizona, New Mexico, and Wyoming. In return, Mexico received US $15,000,000. This exchange is known as the Mexican Cession. Mexicans living in the conquered lands could choose to return to Mexico or stay and become American citizens. Article X was stricken from the treaty before it was ratified by the U.S. Senate. These articles promised that the United States would recognize Mexican and Spanish land grants.

In 1853, in what became known as The Gadsden Purchase, the United States paid an additional $10 million to Mexico to purchase land in what is now southern Arizona and southern New Mexico for the construction of a southern route for a transcontinental railroad. The purchase was also designed to further compensate Mexico for the lands taken by the U.S. after the Mexican-American War.

Mexico lost more than 500,000 square miles (1,300,000 square km) of land, almost half of its territory. The annexed territories contained about 1,000 Mexican families in California and 7,000 in New Mexico. A few moved back to Mexico; the great majority remained in the US, though they were denied citizenship.

A month before the end of the war, Polk was criticized in a United States House of Representatives amendment to a bill praising Major General Zachary Taylor for "a war unnecessarily and unconstitutionally begun by the President of the United States." This criticism, in which Congressman Abraham Lincoln played an important role, followed congressional scrutiny of the war's beginnings, including factual challenges to claims made by President Polk. The vote followed party lines, with all Whigs supporting the amendment. Lincoln's attack haunted his future campaigns in the heavily Democratic state of Illinois, and was cited by enemies well into his presidency. The stand did not cost Lincoln his Congressional seat in Illinois' Seventh Congressional District; the district was the only place in Illinois where a Whig could win high office, and party leaders agreed to one-term limits for Whig representatives there. Lincoln was succeeded by a Democrat, but the Seventh Congressional District voted for Zachary Taylor, a Whig, that fall.

In much of the United States, victory and the acquisition of new land brought a surge of patriotism (the country had also acquired the southern half of the Oregon Country in 1846 through a treaty with Great Britain). Victory seemed to fulfill citizens' belief in their country's Manifest Destiny. While Whig Ralph Waldo Emerson rejected war "as a means of achieving America's destiny," he accepted that "most of the great results of history are brought about by discreditable means." Although the Whigs had opposed the war, they made Zachary Taylor their presidential candidate in the election of 1848, praising his military performance while muting their criticism of the war itself.

It appears the Mexicans of today, true to their built in "no responsibility" character traits of fiesta and siesta lifestyle are responding to Mexican outlaw organizations such as MEChA, OLA, La Raza, Unida Party,and Nation of Aztlan, all spewing forth treasonous poison chanting "Death to America", and "Kill the Gringos". The "Benedict Arnolds" in America, more specifically, the lobotomy brained college "trained" morons with their weak childlike minds, have no concept of the depth of degradation to which their miniscule fried egg brains have degenerated. This is a proved fact the moment they repeat parrot like, the same filth and threats spewed from the mouths of Mexican sedition traitors preaching death to American pigs! Ironically, the very fact this tripe vomited out by the above criminals is not grounds for jail time by American authorities depicts dramatically the crummy and degraded Americans in our government who have abandoned America. Every adult is familiar with the term "Fifth Columnist" as referring to internal groups in a country attempting through subterfuge, lies and treachery, to cause the collapse of that nation. In America, the large majority of our own government elected personnel is participating as a member of a gang to overthrow

America through amnesty for millions of illegal immigrants, inciting riots, murder of American citizens, destruction of the infrastructure, exposing thousands of Americans to terrible injury, horrible deaths on defective roads, collapsing dams, and disease and plague from overpopulation, air borne carriers and contaminated water. This one act will destroy America more effectively than can any military force. All one has to do is read the latest American Society of Civil Engineers report on the United States infrastructure and realize the desperate situation in which most of the pieces of crap comprising our government have placed the American people and America. America has been betrayed and Real Americans getting the shaft while billions of TAX Dollars are dedicated and allocated to lousy Illegal Immigrants. The proper procedure for Real Americans is to institute impeachment procedures Immediately!

Jonesboro, Tennessee:

It has been reported that a large crowd estimated at over 500 Hispanics marched ranting and raving through the streets of Jonesborough with their usual incoherent dumb demands! It is the same old pitch fed by communistic rabble rousers to misled ignorant people who have no knowledge of the real facts and speak like trained parrots. The laws of America are totally defied and ignored while officials stand around with their usual dumb expressions of cowardice and their fingers up their....! Most cities require parade/demonstration permits from American citizens but from Hispanics – nothing. Yellow belly traitors officials in almost every town – what happened to real men?

The demonstrators want changes in the law that would allow millions of aliens here illegally to become U.S. citizens. Many call current laws unfair, saying they pay taxes too. But most in the Tri-Cities think illegal immigrants don't deserve special treatment. More innate stupidity by dumb and cowardly officials mistakenly believed to be trustworthy but in reality – traitors and scumbags!

A poll was conducted later asking, "Should illegal immigrants be allowed to stay in the United States?" Of nearly 300 viewers, a whopping 88 percent say no - Illegal immigrants should not be in the United States. This is even after the local area newspaper and much of the national press deliberately lied and called it immigration. This points out the inherent stupidity of most media retards. They have their rose colored glasses on and the word INVASION looks like immigration! The yellow belly lying media are mostly socialistic and communistic and think they will be immune if Mexicans take over. Think again – the ignorant hordes tell them everyday: "we will kill Gringos and take your property" but the cocky and stupid media fools do not believe it.

Here is the law regarding illegal entry into the United States of America, any person or persons who;

- Enters or attempts to enter the United States at any time or place other than as designated by immigration officers; or

- Eludes examination or inspection by immigration officers; or

- Attempts to enter or obtains entry to the United States by a willfully false or misleading representation or the willful concealment of a material fact; has committed a federal crime. Violations are punishable by criminal fines and imprisonment for up to six months. Repeat offenses can bring up to two years in prison. Additional civil fines may be imposed at the discretion of immigration judges, but civil fines do not negate the criminal sanctions or nature of the offense.

  By all definitions they are criminals. The correct term is illegal alien. It is a lamentable fact that so many newspapers are being traitorous in their stories due to refusal to label illegal aliens as illegal aliens breaking the laws of the United States.

What about it Arnold and George? Is the above a lie or truth? We're waiting for a truthful answer!

A liberal think tank, has released a study that claims deportation is too expensive to be pursued as a realistic option in addressing America's illegal immigration crisis. According to the center, it would cost more than $41 billion annually - roughly $7 billion more than the entire budget for the Department of Homeland Security - to implement an effective deportation program.

The center, as are most liberal far-out mentalities, full of crap. If these idiots had but taken time to add up the costs reported by seven states for one year in direct costs, (free medical) bankruptcies and job losses, the figure would exceed the total cost of loading these arrogant "kill gringos" pieces of crap mentalities in cattle trucks and dump 'em on the Mexico side of the border. Enough is enough!

Please, @#$%^&*, what does the word comprehensive mean other than complete and encompassing. The entire operation would not exceed the cost of Arnold Schwarzenegger's $40 -50 billion per year in California where the latest assessment says one new school will be needed every day for the foreseeable future! Add that up plus all the other goodies demanded and crime and prison costs. Actually, $50 billion a year would be a bargain for America until the garbage cleanup is complete!

Whether deporting the estimated 10 - 20 million illegal aliens in this country might cost as much as the center calculates, the more critical issue is whether, in the face of certain terrorism efforts can the U.S. effectively monitor its borders. The very fact there is such discrepancies in the number of illegal immigrant criminals in America is a condemnation of the incompetence of INS and Homeland Security jaybirds who prove every day they don't know it from a hole in the ground!

More than 250 million people enter America annually from a mind-numbing list of countries. Most of these visitors come and go with no problem. Yet as we experienced on 9/11, some are intent on destroying all that America stands for. America can no longer be the breadbasket of the world!

More than 11 million trucks come across our borders each year, and some 51,000 foreign ships call at our ports. Such numbers remind us that no nation can be totally safe. America, after all, is not a fortress. Especially with G. Bush at the helm!

But that doesn't mean we can't or shouldn't make our borders more secure. Having to deport thousands of border violators is a dead giveaway that our politicians are weak ineffective traitors.

The Constitution authorizes Congress to establish a uniform rule of naturalization and it has done so. The problem is, millions of illegal aliens are thumbing their noses at the law, many of them with the active help of unscrupulous employers.(Big Business Racketeers). If domestic employers faced stiffer, surer sanctions for knowingly hiring illegals, much of this problem would disappear practically overnight. This is more proof of the dirty low down activities of politicians who deliberately ignore this treason!

It is the current ability of undocumented aliens to blend into the work world that sustains illegal immigration. Absent the ability to secure gainful employment, illegal aliens would have no choice but to return to their country of origin.

Deportation of illegal aliens would undoubtedly be expensive, but then, the American taxpayer is currently funding a costly web of social services such as schools, clinics, hospitals and other facilities estimated to be $90 billion to $100 Billion and bankruptcies of medical care facilities caused by illegal criminals demanding – and getting – free services Real Americans are denied. Real smart, and clearly demonstrates the idiocy and incompetence of Political Correctness - the devil incarnate in America. Deportation is the only answer. Get 'em out of America – now! Whatever it takes!!

There is no liberal or conservative way to patrol our nation's borders, only a right way and a wrong way. The same is true of immigration. America is as strong and vibrant as it is because of its immigrant past. But illegal immigration is a criminal act and shouldn't be tolerated simply because enforcing the law against it is costly.

Any government's first, and greatest, responsibility begins with protecting its own territorial integrity, its own borders, no matter what the price.

That thousands of people across the country have taken to the streets to protest a proposed crackdown on illegal immigration should come as no surprise to anyone familiar with America's wink-and-nod attitude on border security by yellow belly crud officials who run and hide (Again continuing rotten treason by the Home Security Department who can really get tough on Border Agents and deputies who do their duty) –sickening! It's a good bet many of these protestors seen defiantly waving Mexican flags on televised news programs are, in fact, here illegally. This is also what they like to do best - demonstrate rather than construct.

Any treasonable approved recommendation for Amnesty by the questionable mentality of most Senate members on the controversial subject of illegal immigration will ignite a fire of resentment that will reach immense proportions. Contrary to a House-passed bill that focuses on border enforcement, the Senate bill would allow illegals to stay here while applying for citizenship and would not punish their unlawful entry as a felony. To reasonably intelligent people giving millions of criminals and their unscrupulous employers what amounts to amnesty is breaking the law and traitorous irresponsibility. With Teddy Kennedy and McCain and their scared conspiring cohorts this is to be expected! What's fair about ignoring the law? Give these traitors the boot to the gutter where they belong!

Below is the list of Senators who voted AGAINST the American people and FOR Illegal Immigrant Amnesty for Criminals. Remember these names when you go to the polls and in the meantime use the addresses below to give them a piece of your mind. They are giving you and your family the shaft so they deserve no better! Congratulations are in order for those Senators who voted against Amnesty for Criminals. The same traitors lied to Americans in 1986 saying there would be no more amnesty and look what we have here – more lies and more millions of Illegal Immigrant Criminals sucking up your futures.

According to a Government Accountability Office (GAO) report, illegal aliens now account for at least 5 percent of the nation's work force, or approximately 11 million people. Worse, various public agencies and private groups agree that at least 850,000 illegals enter America each year, and many stay here. No surprise there, especially considering the federal government's ever-lessening commitment to enforcing immigration law – thanks to George Bush.

Consider: In 1999, the federal government filed more than 400 notices that it intended to fine companies employing illegal aliens. In 2004, the latest year complete figures are available, the GAO found that only three such notices were filed. Obviously, our government excels at counting illegals as they come in, but can't quite get its hands around interdicting them or deporting them.

Illegal immigration isn't something that happens just in Texas, California and a few other border states. The Immigration and Naturalization Service estimates there were 46,000 illegal aliens residing in Tennessee as of 2000. That figure represents more than a 400 percent increase over 1990. The Governor needs to be pressured to rectify this typical yellow belly political performance by fining companies hiring illegals $10,000 per day.

Since 2001, the number of illegals in Tennessee has likely grown considerably due to a spectacular and stupid program to award driving certificates to illegal aliens. (The idiot who came up with this idea should have been strangled at birth). Earlier this year, federal officials uncovered sophisticated black market shuttles carrying South American and Central American illegals from as far away as New Jersey to Tennessee licensing centers, where they have obtained driving licenses and driving certificates on the strength of fake claims of residency.

There's no way to know how many illegals have abused the system in this way, but it's a matter of record that Tennessee has issued more than 51,000 driving certificates since the legislature approved them. The rationale was that illegals were going to drive anyway and that it was better to allow them to take a driver's test and be licensed so they at least became familiar with the rules of the road. Fortunately, the scandal over the black market shuttles has finally scuttled the program.

Each year, more than 250 million people enter America from a mind-numbing list of countries. Most of these visitors come and go with no problem. Yet as the events of Sept. 11 demonstrated, some are intent on destroying all that America stands for. Others want a better life, but don't want to wait to enter the country legally.

More than 11 million trucks come across our borders each year, and some 51,000 foreign ships call at our ports. Such numbers remind us that no nation can be totally safe. America, after all, is not a fortress. But that doesn't mean we can't or shouldn't make our borders more secure. Deportation is an admission that our borders are not as secure as they should be. However, strengthening immigration law, as is now being debated in Congress, means nothing if the government isn't willing to back up its words with action. George Bush will have to be kicked out of the way first!

The Constitution of the United States already authorizes Congress to establish a uniform rule of naturalization, and it has done so. The problem is, millions of illegal aliens are thumbing their noses at the law, many of them with the active help of unscrupulous employers. Get-tough rhetoric on border security is all well and good, but if domestic employers really faced stiffer, surer sanctions for knowingly hiring illegals, much of this problem would disappear practically overnight. It is, after all, the ability of undocumented aliens to blend into the work world that sustains illegal immigration. Absent the ability to secure gainful employment, illegal aliens would have no choice but to return to their country of origin.

It is past time for our political hacks to cease and desist from licking the boots of big business racketeers and work for America and her Real American citizens for a change. As stated before, the low wages paid Illegal Immigrant workers translates into millions of bonus dollars for company officials. We can only surmise how much of this crooked money is deposited in other accounts in appreciation.

Most of the aversion that some native-born Americans have to certain kinds of menial labor is justifiable due to the lousy wages and working conditions. If illegal aliens are willing to work at wages far less than their American counterparts and to live in substandard conditions, that is an indictment of certain unscrupulous employers, – Big Business Racketeers sponsored and protected by political favors - not of American workers in general

But beyond the long-term harm that a wholesale disregard of immigration law is clearly doing, especially to border states which must pick up enormous tabs for medical and other services, it's an obvious injustice to law-abiding Hispanic citizens and all other Americans of Hispanic heritage who came to this country legally, and who value the system of justice and the laws that were meant to provide fair treatment for all!

There is no liberal or conservative way to patrol our nation's borders, only a right way and a wrong way. The same is true of immigration. America is as strong and vibrant as it is because of its immigrant past. But illegal immigration is a criminal act and shouldn't be tolerated simply because enforcing the law against it is difficult or costly; if so, what other laws should go unenforced? Any government's first, and greatest, responsibility begins with protecting its own territorial integrity, its own borders, no matter the hardship, no matter the price.

Demanding U.S. citizenship for illegal immigrants, hundreds of thousands of people have taken to the streets in recent days in demonstrations across the country, including one march in nearby Jonesborough. These events have been staged in the apparent belief that their sheer mass will sway public sentiment and political support in much the same way civil rights marchers in the 1960s helped change the lives of black Americans. The analogy is an alluring one, but fundamentally flawed.

The issues at the heart of blacks' epic struggle for basic human dignity - voting rights, access to employment, even shelter and food - have nothing in common with the so-called "plight" of illegal immigrants. The civil rights movement was, at base, a challenge to American citizens, black and white alike, to rededicate themselves to a common set of core values.

By contrast, illegal immigrants are engaged in a cynical campaign not merely to excuse their own conduct, but to substitute one value for another. In doing so they are attempting to recast their crass economic self-interest as a moral imperative, one that U.S. citizens are supposed to acknowledge with an open heart and an equally open wallet. Such is the politically correct penitence required these days of an America that is apparently too wealthy to be resisted by its poor neighbor to the south.

But, being stupid neglects some inconvenient facts about today's illegal immigrants. Unlike African-Americans, their ancestors were not kidnapped from their homes by slave traders and shipped, against their will, to another country to work in perpetual servitude. Every adult illegal alien in this country is here by stealing his way in. By definition, such individuals move, shadow-like, through the economy, avoiding almost all of the taxes upon which our local, state and federal governments depend to provide everything from area schools to Social Security. American citizens who conspire to evade their taxes in such a flagrant manner are typically fined and imprisoned.

The work ethic of illegal immigrants is often praised, as though this somehow balances their unlawful entry and presence in this country. But legal immigrants work hard, too, as do tens of millions of Americans who were born here. The main difference between illegal immigrants and other workers, obviously, is that illegal immigrants aren't contributing their fair share to the public programs and institutions that sustain this nation. Just as bad, they're lowering wages for young workers and those with entry-level skills. A recent Harvard University study calculates the presence of illegal immigrants artificially depresses wages nationwide for those on the lowest economic rungs of the job world by a whopping 8 percent.

It's also frequently alleged that illegal immigrants are critical to the survival of America's agribusiness, especially in states like California. But if illegals are being drawn into a vacuum created by domestic labor shortages, why do Labor Department statistics show that real wages for farm workers have actually declined since the late 1980s? Contrary to popular mythology, this isn't an industry plagued by labor shortages. Rather, the largely stagnant, even declining wages of farm workers illustrate all too clearly the unmistakable sign of a surfeit of available labor.

In any case, if agribusiness in California can only be sustained by vast federal subsidies, controversial interstate irrigation efforts and an unceasing supply of poorly paid illegals, let's stop artificially propping up that broken system. A far less expensive and more ethical alternative would be to let the free market work as it should. In the end, that would likely mean that we would stop importing illegals from Mexico and allow them to start exporting the low-cost agricultural products they could raise in their own country.

It's also claimed that American consumers save money on a host of products and services illegal immigrants provide but the real savings are pocketed by big business racketeers paying dirt low wages and ripping America off to the tune of hundreds of millions of dollars! But such savings are a proverbial drop in the bucket compared to the higher taxes the rest of us pay for public services that are provided FREE to illegals.

America is a nation of immigrants. But it is also a nation of laws. Immigrants who obey the law and enter this country legally have and always will be welcome.

That said, it is arrogant beyond measure that illegal immigrants would organize demonstrations in this country to protest their "rights." Illegal immigrants have broken the law merely by being here. They have no "rights," but are here at our forbearance.

The integrity and intelligence of the American people are being impugned and sneered at by traitorous political hacks who have no guts or backbone to enforce immigration laws already on the books. Now they are faced with living up to their sworn oath of office –see below – or face the ire of Real Americans and possibility of justifiable anarchy against a rotten government!

Oath required by the Constitution and by Law to be taken by Government officials when taking office:

I,_A,B_, do solemnly swear or (affirm) that I will support and defend the Constitution of the United States against all enemies, foreign and domestic, that I will bear true faith and allegiance to the same, that I take this obligation freely, without any mental reservation or purpose of evasion; and that I will well and faithfully discharge the office of which I am about to enter

So Help Me God!

Lying and betrayal of a sworn oath on the Bible is an impeachable offense! This applies to any and all government officials from President to Congressmen!

Based on performance evidence, impeachment is in order for many Senators and Congressmen and is forthcoming!

Representative Dana Rohrabacher R-Cailif. Is investigating and hot on the trail of lying betraying city and state officials who are in bed with Illegal Immigrant Criminals and perhaps some Mexican Officials – where is the nearest hanging tree? Representative Rohrabacher has asked his colleague to hold hearings to investigate the involvement of the Mexican government in the decision to prosecute Texas Deputy Sheriff Gilmer Hernandez and Border Patrol agents Ignacio Ramos and Jose Compean for shooting incidents involving illegal immigrants.

Rep. Dana Rohrabacher, R-Calif., said his office is writing a memo to Rep. William Delahunt, D-Mass., after disclosing the involvement of the Mexican Consulate in both cases.

"It appears we are bowing more to directions from Mexican government officials than we are to the dictates of our own Constitution and the security of the people of the United States," Rohrabacher said.

The congressman is the ranking Republican member of the Subcommittee on International Organizations, Human Rights, and

Oversight of the House Foreign Affairs Committee. Delahunt has taken Rohrabacher's place as chairman.

Rohrabacher expressed anger that Ramos and Compean are currently in federal prison.

"The only reason these two Border Patrol agents are in federal prison today," he said in an interview "is because of a mean-spirited president who wants to squash people like a bug if they do anything that contradicts his open border policy."

Rohrabacher added, "We have to make sure we save the lives of agents Ramos and Compean. This is our first priority. These two brave heroes are now in jeopardy and their lives are at risk."

As previously reported over the U.S. Ramos was beaten in the federal prison by a group of inmates believed to be Hispanic illegal immigrants, following the TV broadcast of an "America's Most Wanted" show that featured a segment on the case.

"The president has things all mixed up," Rohrabacher said. "We're supposed to side with the law enforcement officers, not the drug dealers. We're supposed to be interested in the security of our borders in order to protect American citizens rather than to make Mexican government officials happy."

Last month, Rohrabacher obtained a ticket for Monica Ramos, the wife of the imprisoned Border Patrol agent, to attend Bush's State of the Union Message.

  Also, a comment made by Rep. Duncan Hunter, R–Calif., firmly opposed to Illegal Immigration, issued an e-mail saying the revelations about Mexican involvement "raise more questions about the validity of the conviction and reaffirm why a review of the case is necessary immediately."

"Too many questions have been raised to allow this conviction to stand without a close and unbiased review," the statement said. It appears from the sleazy actions of local officials who hasten to prosecute law enforcement personnel, that the Mexican government may be involved in making an example of these loyal Americans performing their rightful duty in order to discourage others from resisting the outrageous and illegal acts of foreign criminal trash. Sometimes following the money trail can bring to light many interesting facts. Perhaps prison for officials instead of loyal employees may stop the insane betrayal of America.

In Rock Springs, Texas the sentencing of Officer Hernandez, a city deputy, to prison for defending not only himself from being seriously injured or killed, but attempting to maintain law and order for the citizens, emphasizes the cowardice and willingness of elected officials to abandon the people they represent and crawl over to the side of law breakers under the false claim of protecting the so-called "rights" of Illegal Immigrant Criminals. This is the most absurd abandonment of SWORN duty imaginable. (Perhaps looking a little further into this situation will shed light on the REAL reason for this unwarranted persecution of a loyal police officer). The crummy pieces of crap Mexican Illegal Immigrants had the nerve to claim their civil rights were violated when they tried to run officer Hernandez down and he fired at their vehicle to keep from getting killed. Anyone who believes the lies of obvious Mexican trash criminals has to have slop for brains!

Jimmy Parks, defense attorney for Hernandez, said the unlawful lawsuit "has just become standard operating procedure down here on the border." The fact that a supposed court of law would not throw such obvious lying crap out is extremely disturbing and brings doubt in the belief of honest justice in America!

"There is a natural progression that begins when these people organize a professional (human) smuggling ring to get illegal aliens into the United States," he said. "They become very sophisticated at it, then when law enforcement makes the attempt to try to break up the smuggling ring, they just run away." …

Hernandez was sentenced last week to one-year plus one-day in federal prison for criminally violating the civil rights of the illegal aliens who were in a van that attempted to run over Hernandez after a traffic stop April 14, 2005, in Rocksprings, Texas. …

Parks said the illegal aliens organizing human smuggling operations don't view the lights going off on a police vehicle as "a stop command."

The way to win the lottery is to take off and refuse to obey the lawful authority in the United States, he said. "The illegal aliens know that if they can scrutinize the acts of the law enforcement officer, there's a decent chance the police may end up going to prison, while the illegal aliens end up with one good lawsuit especially when rotten authorities participate in the lying persecution blatantly and arrogantly trying to impress everybody with their illegal authority!

The townspeople of Rocksprings, Texas and all towns and cities bordering stinking lousy Mexico should ask themselves this question: "Why would anyone in their right mind want to be a law enforcement officer in any lousy town this day and age when stinking low down traitorous officials have no integrity and character and parade hand in hand with foreign criminals! Perhaps even better would be for all police to resign and let the rotten illegal immigrant criminals demonstrate their genuine innate character by burning, robbing, rape, and murdering at will. (It is almost that bad now). Cowardly officials should be dragged from under their desks and get their just deserts.

 Hernandez and his family could be ruined financially for life by this treasonous betrayal of so-called authorities. It is mind boggling to attempt to determine the motive behind such persecution and abandonment of any personal courage and national pride. Apparently these type of people have never read historical accounts of what happens to traitors when the barbarians take over – they are the first ones to be killed. Any attempt to kiss up to barbarians is met with contempt and murder.

 A Republican congressman is asking a Democrat colleague to hold hearings to investigate the involvement of the Mexican government in the decision to prosecute Texas Deputy Sheriff Gilmer Hernandez and Border Patrol agents Ignacio Ramos and Jose Compean for shooting incidents involving illegal immigrants.

Another Congressman said - It looks as if certain American officials – in high and low positions are caving in to outrageous claims and lies from Mexican government officials. The dictates of our own Constitution and the security of the people of the United States is being abandoned in the name of insane no guts Political Correctness.

The congressman is one of the top Republican members of the Subcommittee on International Organizations, Human Rights, and Oversight of the House Foreign Affairs Committee. Congressman Delahunt has taken Rohrabacher's place as chairman.

The congressman said he was pleased to see the transcript of the Ramos-Compean trial finally available, some 11 months after the conclusion of the trial.

"Now that we have the transcript of the trial," Rohrabacher said, "the case can go to an appellate judge who can overturn Judge Kathleen Cardone's decision to imprison Ramos and Compean while they appeal the conviction."

Make a note to contact the traitorous lawmakers attempting to push Amnesty for Illegal Immigrants down the throats of Real Americans. The names are listed below!

It appears the United States Senate is set to betray America once again with lies and no guts.

Now, we face the second wave of amnesty-a late night "compromise" hashed out between Majority Leader Frist and Sens. Hagel and Martinez. (More lying, deceit and betrayal of Real Americans because of Fear?) Fear of what? If our Police and Military can't take care of these ignorant illegals then perhaps the betrayed citizens of America can. Failure to haul this trash back to Mexico is inviting anarchy in America! The Real American citizens are not afraid to fight for America if forced into a corner by yellow bellied rotten politicians proposing amnesty for Illegal Criminals who openly state they will kill all the Gringos! How about this Mr. Bush?

Majority Leader Frists new "compromise" allows illegal aliens who have been here for at least five years (Illegally) to have AMNESTY. (More lying crapola – how do these BB Brain people get elected)?

Those who recently entered the country have only to apply for papers and get legal status, and the requirement they depart the country is full of loopholes, starting with the fact this "mandatory" measure can be waived. Thus, the longer you've broken the law the greater your reward. Does anyone believe that this scenario is any better? Document fraud has become a bigger business than money counterfeiting and is accepted by big business racketeers without question in their rotten low down betrayal of Real Americans to be able to continue to implement their personal fraud and greed for big corporate profits and bonuses!

Amnesty by any other name is still Amnesty. Amnesty proposed by our politicians is like jumping from the frying pan into the fire- remember the lying promises of the 1986 bunch who guaranteed there would never be any more? Lies and more Lies! The leader of this travesty was none other than Mr. Teddy Kennedy – surprised? Amnesty is like a magnet to Illegal Immigrants who could care less they are destroying livelihoods of Americans and rush unimpeded to the Southwest cities, all with the tacit approval of G. Bush who says one thing and does something entirely different. How can Americans have faith and trust in a President who will not be up front about his real immigration program. Illegal Immigrants make a mockery of U.S immigration laws. And amnesties beget more amnesties. The 1986 amnesty was a disaster drawing in about three fold more illegal immigrants. This amnesty is at least a dozen times larger in scope than the 1986 amnesty. It would be a colossal disaster. It would bury the Republican Party in just a few years. That's why most of the Democrats are voting for it.

More Direct Arrogant disregard for the 80% of Real Americans who are against Illegal Immigration and any form of Amnesty is shown below. The names shown below voted Amnesty for Illegal Immigrant

Criminals and is totally against the will of Real Americans! Is this not treason against the will of the people? Who will Real Americans vote for in the next elections – certainly not for these cowards who have nothing but contempt for loyal freedom loving Americans. In the meantime impeachment proceedings should be under way for all on this list!

Senators Voting For
Illegal Immigrant Amnesty

Akaka (D-HI)

Baucus (D-MT)

Bayh (D-IN)

Bennett (R-UT)

Biden (D-DE)

Bingaman (D-NM)

Boxer (D-CA)

Brownback (R-KS)

Cantwell (D-WA)

Carper (D-DE)

Chafee (R-RI)

*** Clinton (D-NY)

Coleman (R-MN)

Collins (R-ME)

Conrad (D-ND)

Craig (R-ID)

Dayton (D-MN)

DeWine (R-OH)

Dodd (D-CT)

Domenici (R-NM)

Durbin (D-IL)

Feingold (D-WI)

Feinstein (D-CA)

Frist (R-TN)

Graham (R-SC

Gregg (R-NH)

Hagel (R-NE)

Harkin (D-IA)

Inouye (D-HI)

Jeffords (I-VT)

Johnson (D-SD)

Kennedy (D-MA)

Kerry (D-MA)

Kohl (D-WI)

Landrieu (D-LA)

Lautenberg (D-NJ)

Leahy (D-VT)

Levin (D-MI)

Lieberman (D-CT)

Lincoln (D-AR)

Lugar (R-IN)

Martinez (R-FL)

*** McCain (R-AZ)

McConnell (R-KY)

Menendez (D-NJ)

Mikulski (D-MD)

Murkowski (R-AK)

Murray (D-WA)

Nelson (D-FL)

***Obama (D-IL)

Pryor (D-AR)

Reed (D-RI)

Reid (D-NV)

Sarbanes (D-MD)

Schumer (D-NY)

Smith (R-OR)

Snowe (R-ME)

Specter (R-PA)

Stevens (R-AK)

Voinovich (R-OH)

Warner (R-VA)

Wyden (D-OR)

*** And these American deserters want to be president?

With friends like these who needs enemies?

Give 'em the old Heave Ho out in the street!

It is good news to hear that Immigration and Customs Enforcement (ICE) has raided six meat packing plants owned by Swift & Co. leading to bus loads of illegal aliens being arrested. While some speculate a possible relationship exists, there is no indication of a relationship between this raid and concerns over the outbreaks of food born diseases at this time. It is general policy for companies that stoop to hiring illegals to not bother checking for transmittable disease and thus are more likely responsible for food contamination across the nation.

This raid alss claimed dozens of charges of identity theft. Activists have been calling for identity theft charges in the case with Smithfield Foods Inc. and their many illegal alien workers. This is Treason! Perhaps there will be some justice now for the American families facing the nightmare of identity theft caused by these illegal aliens and the company that gave them jobs!

This outrage supports the earlier statement that the United States of America is the most corrupt nation on the face of the earth.

According to several surveys, riots and protests by illegal aliens could be worse than or equal to the violence in France, and could happen soon in America. Another 14% feel such riots could take place here but with less damage.

There is no reason or excuse to wait until Illegal Immigrant morons start to riot. The only solution to keep America free is to load them into cattle trucks for a trip back to lousy Mexico!

Enough is enough and our cowardly politicians had better wake up and get with the only acceptable solution – hauling 12 - 18 million illegals back to their rotten homeland.

Again: Enough is Enough.

Mexican trash has the gall to threaten U.S. Police officers –and they are illegal criminals. It appears the officers will have to change tactics over rule yellow officials and use force to get rid of these arrogant pieces of crap.

Take a hard look at these two quotes closely as they reflect a trend much deeper than one or two angry illegal alien supporters.

It was reported that as the buses left, a thinning crowd of 150-200 shouted at Greeley police officers assigned to help control the area. One piece of stupid crap yelled in the face of police: "We're not going to take this anymore. This is our country!"

Arrogant crowds pushed down part of a barricade near the entrance to the plant, until SWAT team forces arrived.

Here is a perfect example of the arrogance and evil intent to take over America with cooperation by traitorous political officials: Andres Guerrero, who teaches Spanish at Aims Community College, joined the protesters. He said, "In ten years we're going to take over the southland, trust me." "This is our land and always will be our land."

This piece of crap is a lying SOB – The land belonged to the Indians first. Mexico started the war, the United States whipped the crap out of them, Mexico signed over the territory and the U.S. gave them a check for $15 Million dollars. (One Billion Dollars today's money!)

Big Question: Are Real Americans to stand by and put up with this crap of direct threats to take over America or do we stop it by whatever means necessary? Don't take this threat lightly, these people (animals) are deadly serious about wresting control of territory from the United States because, and here is the kicker: they have seen the lack of guts and dedication demonstrated by the majority of politicians sworn to protect America from enemies, Foreign and Domestic. Having experienced the whining and begging attitude of those responsible for the safety and security of America, Illegal Immigrant Criminals have no fear of retaliation and continue on their march to take over America while "Fiddling While Rome Burns" has become the theme song of our gutless politicians.

Someone with true perspicacity coined a phrase long ago which applies 100% to our rotten political structure in the United States: "Politicians Are Liars and Thieves. Most will tell unholy lies to get elected and proceed to steal the gold fillings out of your teeth!" Is it any wonder America is sliding to oblivion down a runway greased by the oily tongues of the majority of our politicians.

The state of California is a prime example of promises by a politician and actual typical performance. Mr. "Hero" Arnold Schwarzenegger should show Real American citizens his tongue for verification that it is forked:

1. Supports John McCain's bill # S1461 which will completely destroy America!

2. Wants to legitimize undocumented illegal immigrants.

3. Is promoting a coalition of other border states hoping to exert pressure on the Federal Government for billions in order to support <u>Demands</u> by Illegals.

4. Repeated numerous times during campaign that he would follow wishes of legitimate citizens – but lied and instead is holding out a welcoming hand to vicious gangs of Hispanic animals!

5. Spending an estimated $30 – $40 Billion dollars to support Illegal Immigrants and gangs terrorizing citizens. HELLO!?@#%*&. Let's hear your lying denials Arnold!

6. Handcuffing law enforcement efforts and risking safety and lives of Real American Citizens! by ordering officials to not bother the criminals. This is grounds for impeachment and Californians better get busy and kick the "Movie Hero" out into the gutter.

Some of the most violent criminals at large today are illegal aliens. Yet in cities where the crime these aliens commit is highest, the police cannot use the most obvious tool to apprehend them: their immigration status. In Los Angeles, for example, dozens of members of a ruthless Salvadoran prison gang have sneaked back into town after having been deported for such crimes as murder, assault with a deadly weapon, and drug trafficking. Police officers know who they are and know that their mere presence in the country is a felony. Yet should a cop arrest an illegal gangbanger for felonious reentry, it is he who will be treated as a criminal, for violating the LAPD's rule against enforcing immigration law. The traitors who are behind the giveaway of America need to be killed, not innocent American citizens who trusted these treasonous Ass h**es and were murdered, raped and tortured as a reward for their trust!

The LAPD's ban on immigration enforcement mirrors bans in immigrant-saturated cities around the country, from New York and Chicago to San Diego, Austin, and Houston. These "sanctuary policies" generally prohibit city employees, including the cops, from reporting immigration violations to federal authorities.

Such laws testify to the sheer political power of immigrant lobbies,(should have tgeir as**es run out of town) big business racketeers,(Traitorous SOB's they should be in jail)), that police officials shrink from even mentioning the illegal-alien crime wave. "We can't even talk about it," says a frustrated LAPD captain. "People are afraid of a backlash from Hispanics." – How about naming these people! (The proper response is to blow 'em away like they are threatening to do us –before they do us). Another LAPD commander in a predominantly Hispanic, gang-infested district sighs: "I would get a firestorm of criticism if I talked about [enforcing the immigration law against illegals]." Neither captain would speak for attribution. Rotten cowardly superiors in the pockets of big business racketeers!

Perhaps this would be an ideal time for police forces call for a national strike to stay home and let the yellow cowards giving orders to pacify instead of killing the gang members, take care of their sworn obligation to Real American citizens. Run and hide is their way of protecting Real Americans.

But however pernicious in themselves, sanctuary rules are a symptom of a much broader disease: the nation's near-total loss of control over immigration policy. Fifty years ago, immigration policy might have driven immigration numbers, but today the numbers drive policy. The nonstop increase of immigration is reshaping the language and the law to dissolve any distinction between legal and illegal aliens and, ultimately, the very idea of national borders. This is the reward the majority of our gutless wonder politicians have reaped for America and trusting Real Americans.

It is a measure of how topsy-turvy the immigration environment has become that to ask police officials about the illegal-alien crime problem feels like a gross faux pas, not done in polite company. And a police official asked to violate this powerful taboo will give a strangled response—or, as in the case of a New York deputy commissioner, break off communication altogether. Meanwhile, millions of illegal aliens work, shop, travel, and commit crimes in plain view, utterly secure in their de facto immunity from the immigration law.

Fox News reported the Miami Police Department's spokesman, Detective Delrish Moss, when asked about his employer's policy on lawbreaking illegals offered this information to show, not only the stupidity of city officials but emphasizes their cowardice as well! In September, the force arrested a Honduran visa violator for seven vicious rapes. The previous year, Miami cops had had the suspect in custody for lewd and lascivious molestation, without checking his immigration status. Had they done so, they would have discovered his visa violation, a deportable offense, and so could have forestalled the rapes. "We have shied away from unnecessary involvement dealing with immigration issues," explains Moss, choosing his words carefully, "because of our large immigrant population."

There is no room for a governor to abandon his oath of office and allow criminal gangs to run amok. This is excecutive cowardice at the worst. In fact if one or two of these cowardly officials were impeached, dishonored, and their A**es kicked out in the gutter, perhaps others would get the message, crack down on Mexican gangs and haul 'em back to lousy NAFTA Mexico.

Police commanders may not want to discuss, much less respond to, the illegal-alien crisis, but its magnitude for law enforcement is startling. Some examples:

- In Los Angeles, 95 percent of all outstanding warrants for homicide (which total 1,200 to 1,500) target illegal aliens. Up to two-thirds of all fugitive felony warrants (17,000) are for illegal aliens.

- A confidential California Department of Justice study reported in 1995 that 60 percent of the 20,000-strong 18th Street Gang in southern California is illegal; police officers say the proportion is actually much greater. The bloody gang collaborates with the Mexican Mafia, the dominant force in California prisons, on complex drug-distribution schemes, extortion, and drive-by assassinations, and commits an assault or robbery every day in L.A. County. The gang has grown dramatically over the last two decades by recruiting recently arrived youngsters, most of them illegal, from Central America and Mexico.

- Available data on the leadership of the Columbia Lil' Cycos gang, which uses murder and racketeering to control the drug market around L.A.'s MacArthur Park, was about 60 percent illegal in 2002, says former assistant U.S. attorney Luis Li. Francisco Martinez, a Mexican Mafia member and an illegal alien, controlled the gang from prison, while serving time for felonious reentry following deportation.

Good luck finding any reference to such facts in official crime analysis. The LAPD and the L.A. city attorney recently requested an injunction against drug trafficking in Hollywood, targeting the 18th Street Gang and the "non–gang members" who sell drugs in Hollywood for the gang. Those non–gang members are virtually all illegal Mexicans, smuggled into the country by a ring organized by 18th Street Gangs. The Mexicans pay off their transportation debts to the gang by selling drugs; many soon realize how lucrative that line of work is and stay in the business.

Cops and prosecutors universally know the immigration status of these non-gang "Hollywood dealers," as the city attorney calls them, but the gang injunction is assiduously silent on the matter. And if a Hollywood officer were to arrest an illegal dealer (known on the street as a "border brother") for his immigration status, or even notify the Immigration and Naturalization Service (since early 2003, absorbed into the new Department of Homeland Security), he would face severe discipline for violating Special Order 40, the city's sanctuary policy.

The ordinarily tough-as-nails former LAPD chief Daryl Gates enacted Special Order 40 in 1979—showing that even the most unapologetic law-and-order cop is no match for immigration advocates. The order prohibits officers from "initiating police action where the objective is to discover the alien status of a person"—in other words, the police may not even ask someone they have arrested about his immigration status until after they have filed criminal charges, nor may they arrest someone for immigration violations. They may not notify immigration authorities about an illegal alien picked up for minor violations. Only if they have already booked an illegal alien for a felony or for multiple misdemeanors may they inquire into his status or report him. The insane actions of our lying stupid officials will more than likely be the direct cause of anarchy in the streets of America as Genuine Real American citizens fight to preserve America from takeover and destruction by illegal (multiplying like rats) immigrants who have no interest in law and order or making America a prosperous nation – just kill all gringos and turn America into another lousy filthy Mexico!

L.A.'s sanctuary law and all others like it contradict a key 1990s policing discovery: the Great Chain of Being in criminal behavior. Pick up a law-violator for a "minor" crime, and you might well prevent a major crime: enforcing graffiti and turnstile-jumping laws nabs you murderers and robbers. Enforcing known immigration violations, such as reentry following deportation, against known felons, would be even more productive. LAPD officers recognize illegal deported gang members all the time—flashing gang signs at court hearings for rival gangbangers, hanging out on the corner, or casing a target. These illegal returnees are, simply by being in the country after deportation, committing a felony (in contrast to garden-variety illegals on their first trip to the U.S., say, who are only committing a misdemeanor). "But if I see a deportee from the Mara Salvatrucha [Salvadoran prison] gang crossing the street, I know I can't touch him," laments a Los Angeles gang officer. Only if the deported felon has given the officer some other reason to stop him, such as an observed narcotics sale, can the cop accost him—but not for the immigration felony.

Though such a policy puts the community at risk, the department's top brass brush off such concerns. No big deal if you see deported gangbangers back on the streets, they say. Just put them under surveillance for "real" crimes and arrest them for those. But surveillance is very manpower-intensive. Where there is an immediate ground for getting a violent felon off the street and for questioning him further, it is absurd to demand that the woefully understaffed LAPD ignore it.

The stated reasons for sanctuary policies are that they encourage illegal-alien crime victims and witnesses to cooperate with cops without fear of deportation, and that they encourage illegals to take advantage of city services like health care and education (to whose maintenance few illegals have contributed a single tax dollar, of course). There has never been any empirical verification that sanctuary laws actually accomplish these goals—and no one has ever suggested not enforcing drug laws, say, for fear of intimidating drug-using crime victims. But in any case, this official rationale could be honored by limiting police use of immigration laws to some subset of immigration violators: deported felons, say, or repeat criminal offenders whose immigration status police already know.

The real reason cities prohibit their cops and other employees from immigration reporting and enforcement is, like nearly everything else in immigration policy, the numbers. The immigrant population has grown so large that public officials are terrified of alienating it, even at the expense of ignoring the law and tolerating violence. In 1996, a breathtaking Los Angeles Times exposé on the 18th Street Gang, which included descriptions of innocent bystanders being murdered by laughing cholos (gang members), revealed the rate of illegal-alien membership in the gang. In response to the public outcry, the Los

Angeles City Council ordered the police to reexamine Special Order 40. You would have thought it had suggested reconsidering Roe v. Wade. A police commander warned the council: "This is going to open a significant, heated debate." City Councilwoman Laura Chick put on a brave front: "We mustn't be afraid," she declared firmly.

But of course immigrant pandering trumped public safety. Law-abiding residents of gang-infested neighborhoods may live in terror of the tattooed gangbangers dealing drugs, spraying graffiti, and shooting up rivals outside their homes, but such anxiety can never equal a politician's fear of offending Hispanics. At the start of the reexamination process, LAPD deputy chief John White had argued that allowing the department to work closely with the INS would give cops another tool for getting gang members off the streets. Trying to build a homicide case, say, against an illegal gang member is often futile, he explained, since witnesses fear deadly retaliation if they cooperate with the police. Enforcing an immigration violation would allow the cops to lock up the murderer right now, without putting a witness's life at risk. Evidence of more traitorous cowardly officials.

But six months later, Deputy Chief White had changed his tune: "Any broadening of the policy gets us into the immigration business," he asserted. "It's a federal law-enforcement issue, not a local law-enforcement issue." Interim police chief Bayan Lewis told the L.A. Police Commission: "It is not the time. It is not the day to look at Special Order 40."

Nor will it ever be, as long as immigration numbers continue to grow. After their brief moment of truth in 1996, Los Angeles politicians have only grown more adamant in defense of Special Order 40. After learning that cops in the scandal-plagued Rampart Division had cooperated with the INS to try to uproot murderous gang members from the community, local politicians threw a fit, criticizing district commanders for even allowing INS agents into their station houses. In turn, the LAPD strictly disciplined the offending officers. By now, big-city police chiefs are unfortunately just as determined to defend sanctuary policies as the politicians who appoint them; not so the rank and file, however, who see daily the benefit that an immigration tool would bring.

Immigration politics have similarly harmed New York. Former mayor Rudolph Giuliani sued all the way up to the Supreme Court to defend the city's sanctuary policy against a 1996 federal law decreeing that cities could not prohibit their employees from cooperating with the INS. Oh yeah? said Giuliani; just watch me. The INS, he claimed, with what turned out to be grotesque irony, only aims to "terrorize people." Though he lost in court, he remained defiant to the end. On September 5, 2001, his handpicked charter-revision committee ruled that New York could still require that its employees keep immigration information confidential to preserve trust between immigrants and government. Six days later, several visa-overstayers participated in the most devastating attack on the city and the country in history. It appears Mr. Giuliani does not have the hero status once ascribed to him!

New York conveniently forgot the 1996 federal ban on sanctuary laws until a gang of five Mexicans—four of them illegal—abducted and brutally raped a 42-year-old mother of two near some railroad tracks in Queens. The NYPD had already arrested three of the illegal aliens numerous times for such crimes as assault, attempted robbery, criminal trespass, illegal gun possession, and drug offenses. The department had never notified the INS.

Citizen outrage forced Mayor Michael Bloomberg to revisit the city's sanctuary decree yet again. In May 2003, Bloomberg tweaked the policy minimally to allow city staffers to inquire into immigration status only if it is relevant to the awarding of a government benefit. Though Bloomberg's new rule said nothing about reporting immigration violations to federal officials, advocates immediately claimed that it did allow such reporting, and the ethnic lobbies went ballistic. "What we're seeing is the erosion of people's rights," thundered Angelo Falcon (the usual foreign piece of crap) of the Puerto Rican Legal Defense and Education Fund. After three months of intense agitation by immigrant groups, Bloomberg replaced this innocuous "don't ask" policy with a "don't tell" rule even broader than Gotham's original sanctuary policy – another traitorous SOB). The new rule prohibits city employees from giving other government officials information not just about immigration status but about tax payments, sexual orientation, welfare status, and other matters.

But even were immigrant-saturated cities to discard their sanctuary policies and start enforcing immigration violations where public safety demands it, the resource-starved immigration authorities couldn't handle the overwhelming additional workload.

The chronic shortage of manpower to oversee, and detention space to house, aliens as they await their deportation hearings (or, following an order of removal from a federal judge, their actual deportation) has forced immigration officials to practice a constant triage. Long ago, the feds stopped trying to find and deport aliens who had "merely" entered the country illegally through stealth or fraudulent documents. Currently, the only types of illegal aliens who run any risk of catching federal attention are those who have been convicted of an "aggravated felony" (a particularly egregious crime) or who have been deported following conviction for an aggravated felony and who have reentered (an offense punishable with 20 years in jail).

That triage has been going on for a long time, as former INS investigator Mike Cutler, who worked with the NYPD catching Brooklyn drug dealers in the 1970s, explains. "If you arrested someone you wanted to detain, you'd go to your boss and start a bidding war," Cutler recalls. "You'd say: 'My guy ran three blocks, threw a couple of punches, and had six pieces of ID.' The boss would turn to another agent: 'Next! Whad did your guy do?' 'He ran 18 blocks, pushed over an old lady, and had a gun.' " But such one-upmanship was usually fruitless. "Without the jail space," explains Cutler, "it was like the Fish and Wildlife Service; you'd tag their ear and let them go."

But even when immigration officials actually arrest someone, and even if a judge issues a final deportation order (usually after years of litigation and appeals), they rarely have the manpower to put the alien on a bus or plane and take him across the border. Second alternative: detain him pending removal. Again, inadequate space and staff. In the early 1990s, for example, 15 INS officers were in charge of the deportation of approximately 85,000 aliens (not all of them criminals) in New York City. The agency's actual response to final orders of removal was what is known as a "run letter"—a notice asking the deportable alien kindly to show up in a month or two to be deported, when the agency might be able to process him. Results: in 2001, 87 percent of deportable aliens who received run letters disappeared, a number that was even higher—94 percent—if they were from terror-sponsoring countries.

To other law-enforcement agencies, the feds' triage often looks like complete indifference to immigration violations. Testifying to Congress about the Queens rape by illegal Mexicans, New York's criminal justice coordinator defended the city's failure to notify the INS after the rapists' previous arrests on the ground that the agency wouldn't have responded anyway. "We have time and time again been unable to reach INS on the phone," John Feinblatt said last February. "When we reach them on the phone, they require that we write a letter. When we write a letter, they require that it be by a superior."

Criminal aliens also interpret the triage as indifference. John Mullaly a former NYPD homicide detective, estimates that 70 percent of the drug dealers and other criminals in Manhattan's Washington Heights were illegal. Were Mullaly to threaten an illegal-alien thug in custody that his next stop would be El Salvador unless he cooperated, the criminal would just laugh, knowing that the INS would never show up. The message could not be clearer: this is a culture that can't enforce its most basic law of entry. If policing's broken-windows theory is correct, the failure to enforce even one set of rules breeds overall contempt for the law.

The sheer number of criminal aliens overwhelmed an innovative program that would allow immigration officials to complete deportation hearings while a criminal was still in state or federal prison, so that upon his release he could be immediately ejected without taking up precious INS detention space. But the process, begun in 1988, immediately bogged down due to the numbers— in 2000, for example, nearly 30 percent of federal prisoners were foreign-born. The agency couldn't find enough pro bono attorneys to represent such an army of criminal aliens (who have extensive due-process rights in contesting deportation) and so would have to request delay after delay. Or enough immigration judges would not be available. In 1997, the INS simply had no record of a whopping 36 percent of foreign-born inmates who had been released from federal and four state prisons without any review of their deportability. They included 1,198 aggravated felons, 80 of whom were soon re-arrested for new crimes.

Resource starvation is not the only reason for federal inaction. The INS was a creature of immigration politics, and INS district directors came under great pressure from local politicians to divert scarce resources into distribution of such "benefits" as permanent residency, citizenship, and work permits, and away from criminal or other investigations. In the late 1980s, for example, the INS refused to join an FBI task force against Haitian drug trafficking in Miami, fearing criticism for "Haitian-bashing." In 1997, after Hispanic activists protested a much-publicized raid that netted nearly two dozen illegals, the Border Patrol said that it would no longer join Simi Valley, California, probation officers on home searches of illegal-alien-dominated gangs. Sentencing America to death by cowardice!

The disastrous Citizenship USA project of 1996 was a luminous case of politics driving the INS to sacrifice enforcement to "benefits." When, in the early 1990s, the prospect of welfare reform drove immigrants to apply for citizenship in record numbers to preserve their welfare eligibility, the Clinton administration, seeing a political bonanza in hundreds of thousands of new welfare-dependent citizens, ordered the naturalization process radically expedited. Thanks to relentless administration pressure, processing errors in 1996 were 99 percent in New York and 90 percent in Los Angeles, and tens of thousands of aliens with criminal records, including for murder and armed robbery, were naturalized.

Another powerful political force, the immigration bar association, has won from Congress an elaborate set of due-process rights for criminal aliens that can keep them in the country indefinitely. Federal probation officers in Brooklyn are supervising two illegals—a Jordanian and an Egyptian with Saudi citizenship—who look "ready to blow up the Statue of Liberty," according to a probation official, but the officers can't get rid of them. The Jordanian had been caught fencing stolen Social Security and tax-refund checks; now he sells phone cards, which he uses himself to make untraceable calls. The Saudi's offense: using a fraudulent Social Security number to get employment—a puzzlingly unnecessary scam, since he receives large sums from the Middle East, including from millionaire relatives. But intelligence links him to terrorism, so presumably he worked in order not to draw attention to himself. Currently, he changes his cell phone every month. Ordinarily such a minor offense would not be prosecuted, but the government, fearing that he had terrorist intentions, used whatever it had to put him in prison.

Now, probation officers desperately want to see the duo out of the country, but the two ex-cons have hired lawyers, who are relentlessly fighting their deportation. "Due process allows you to stay for years without an adjudication," says a probation officer in frustration. "A regular immigration attorney can keep you in the country for three years, a high-priced one for ten." In the meantime, Brooklyn probation officials are watching the bridges.

Even where immigration officials successfully nab and deport criminal aliens, the reality, says a former federal gang prosecutor, is that "they all come back. They can't make it in Mexico." The tens of thousands of illegal farm workers and dishwashers who overpower U.S. border controls every year carry in their wake thousands of brutal assailants and terrorists who use the same smuggling industry and who benefit from the same irresistible odds: there are so many more of them than the Border Patrol.

For, of course, the government's inability to keep out criminal aliens is part and parcel of its inability to patrol the border, period. For decades, the INS had as much effect on the migration of millions of illegals as a can tied to the tail of a tiger. And the immigrants themselves, despite the press cliché of hapless aliens living fearfully in the shadows, seemed to regard immigration authorities with all the concern of an elephant for a flea.

Certainly fear of immigration officers is not in evidence among the hundreds of illegal day laborers who hang out on Roosevelt Avenue in Queens, New York, in front of money wire services, travel agencies, immigration-attorney offices, and phone arcades, all catering to the local Hispanic population (as well as to drug dealers and terrorists). "There is no chance of getting caught," cheerfully explains Rafael, an Ecuadoran. Like the dozen Ecuadorans and Mexicans on his particular corner, Rafael is hoping that an SUV seeking carpenters for $100 a day will show up soon. "We don't worry, because we're not doing anything wrong. I know it's illegal; I need the papers, but here, nobody asks you for papers." The Governor should be impeached along with G. Bush!

Even the newly fortified Mexican border, the one spot where the government really tries to prevent illegal immigration, looms as only a minor inconvenience to the day laborers. The odds, they realize, are overwhelmingly in their favor. Miguel, a reserved young carpenter, crossed the border at Tijuana three years ago with 15 others. Border Patrol spotted them, but with six officers to 16 illegals, only five got caught. In illegal border crossings, you get what you pay for, Miguel says. If you try to shave on the fee, the coyotes will abandon you at the first problem. Miguel's wife was flying into New York from Los Angeles that very day; it had cost him $2,200 to get her across the border. "Because I pay, I don't worry," he says complacently.

The only way to dampen illegal immigration and its attendant train of criminals and terrorists—short of an economic revolution in the sending countries or an impregnably militarized border—is to remove the jobs magnet. As long as migrants know they can easily get work, they will find ways to evade border controls. But enforcing laws against illegal labor is among government's lowest priorities. In 2001, only 124 agents nationwide were trying to find and prosecute the hundreds of thousands of employers and millions of illegal aliens who violate the employment laws, the Associated Press reports.

Even were immigration officials to devote adequate resources to worksite investigations, not much would change, because their legal weapons are so weak. That's no accident: though it is a crime to hire illegal aliens, a coalition of libertarians, business lobbies, and left-wing advocates has consistently blocked the fraud-proof form of work authorization necessary to enforce that ban. Libertarians have erupted in hysteria at such proposals as a toll-free number to the Social Security Administration for employers to confirm Social Security numbers. Hispanics warn just as stridently that helping employers verify work eligibility would result in discrimination against Hispanics—implicitly conceding that vast numbers of Hispanics work illegally.

The result: hiring practices in illegal-immigrant-saturated industries are a charade. Millions of illegal workers pretend to present valid documents, and thousands of employers pretend to believe them. The law doesn't require the employer to verify that a worker is actually qualified to work, and as long as the proffered documents are not patently phony—scrawled with red crayon on a matchbook, say—the employer will nearly always be exempt from liability merely by having eyeballed them. To find an employer guilty of violating the ban on hiring illegal aliens, immigration authorities must prove that he knew he was getting fake papers—an almost insurmountable burden. Meanwhile, the market for counterfeit documents has exploded: in one month alone in 1998, immigration authorities seized nearly 2 million of them in Los Angeles, destined for immigrant workers, welfare seekers, criminals, and terrorists.

For illegal workers and employers, there is no downside to the employment charade. If immigration officials ever do try to conduct an industry-wide investigation—which will at least net the illegal employees, if not the employers—local congressmen will almost certainly head it off. An INS inquiry into the Vidalia-onion industry in Georgia was not only aborted by Georgia's congressional delegation; it actually resulted in a local amnesty for the growers' illegal workforce. The downside to complying with the spirit of the employment law, on the other hand, is considerable. Ethnic advocacy groups are ready to picket employers who dismiss illegal workers, and employers understandably fear being undercut by less scrupulous competitors.

Of the incalculable changes in American politics, demographics, and culture that the continuing surge of migrants is causing, one of the most profound is the breakdown of the distinction between legal and illegal entry. Everywhere, illegal aliens receive free public education and free medical care at taxpayer expense; 13 states offer them driver's licenses. States everywhere have been pushed to grant illegal aliens college scholarships and reduced in-state tuition. One hundred banks, over 800 law-enforcement agencies, and dozens of cities accept an identification card created by Mexico to credentialize illegal Mexican aliens in the U.S. The Bush administration (Who is the Bush administration except the man himself – George Bush) - has given its (his) blessing to this matricula consular card, over the strong protest of the FBI, which warns that the gaping security loopholes that the card creates make it a boon to money launderers, immigrant smugglers, and terrorists. Border authorities have already caught an Iranian man sneaking across the border this year, Mexican matricula card in hand. A real smart move Mr. Bush! Well,we know now Mr. Bush is out to destroy the United States with immigration criminals. Apparently impeachment is the only way to get rid of him since it is quite obvious our yellow rotten politicians won't do it.

Hispanic advocates have helped blur the distinction between a legal and an illegal resident by asserting that differentiating the two is an act of irrational bigotry. Arrests of illegal aliens inside the border now inevitably spark protests, often led by the Mexican government, that feature signs calling for "no más racismo." Immigrant advocates use the language of "human rights" to appeal to an authority higher than such trivia as citizenship laws. They attack the term "amnesty" for implicitly acknowledging the validity of borders. Indeed, grouses Illinois congressman Luis Gutierrez, "There's an implication that somehow you did something wrong and you need to be forgiven."

Illegal aliens and their advocates speak loudly about what they think the U.S. owes them, not vice versa. "I believe American citizens have a right . . . to work, to drive their kids to school," said California assemblywoman Sarah Reyes. An immigration agent says that people he stops "get in your face about their rights, because our failure to enforce the law emboldens them." Taking this idea to its extreme, Joaquín Avila, a UCLA Chicano studies professor and law lecturer, argues that to deny non-citizens the vote, especially in the many California cities where they constitute the majority, is a form of apartheid. This is a typical lame brain academic moronic statement. More than likely this traitor would say non citizens (Illegal Criminals) have the RIGHT to riot and kill Americans if they so desire! Tar and Feathers for this imbecile!

America is for Americans – not traitors. Where is the nearest hanging tree?

Yet no poll has ever shown that Americans want more open borders. Quite the reverse. By a huge majority—at least 60 percent—they want to rein in immigration, and they endorse an observation that Senator Alan Simpson made 20 years ago: Americans "are fed up with efforts to make them feel that [they] do not have that fundamental right of any people—to decide who will join them and help form the future country in which they and their posterity will live." But if the elites' and the advocates' idea of giving voting rights to non-citizen majorities catches on—and don't be surprised if it does due to mental constipation and diarrhea of the mouth of sick Americans living in an imaginary perfect world. A non-citizen is an outlaw insofar as voting rights are interpreted. The only guaranteed solution to the Illegal Immigrant nightmare is to "Get the trucks and haul 'em back to Mexico". America will then be 100% more peaceful, safer, increased educational opportunities, better job availability, medical care facilities that will not be bankrupted by insane free service to criminals, and perhaps our outlaw political setup in America can find time to fix the collapsing infrastructure before thousands of citizens are killed by decaying expressways, bridges and dam failures. Professional estimates have placed the cost at $1.6 Trillion which instead will "given" to Illegal Immigrants for free Social Security, new useless school facilities, free social services, food and clothing, and Medical Services – and, as mouthed by many fools in our government and so-called academic circles "all because the poor things deserve our help". In the first place they are in the United States illegally (Criminally). In the second place they are publicly outspoken about killing "Gringos". (This by a professor at Texas University). The fact that this scum made a remark of such contempt and direct threat here in America and is still out of jail speaks volumes as to the decadent situation in today's government! In the third place they claim all of the Southwest United States is their land and they are taking it back.

In the fourth place they will play hell taking this part of America as theirs.

California is the largest crime center in America accommodating the pieces of crap forming gangs to murder, rob and intimidate – even daring police to interfere because traitorous elements in the yellow bellied state government are too scared to protect the Real American citizens of California and have actually ordered police to back off instead of shooting the murderous dirtbags! Who is in charge of this atrocious and insane policy to give America to criminals in the very face of the demonstrations of intent to kill Real Americans? This is a pitiful display and abandonment of sworn duty to protect lives and property of trusting law abiding citizens. Again, where is the tar and feathers. Also, cattle trucks to haul the animals back to Mexico?

The top official in California elected to protect, provide for life, liberty and pursuit of happiness in California is the Governor!

And this person is? Mr. Arnold Schwarzenegger

The law provides for redress of grievances by betrayed citizens known as IMPEACHMENT! It's past time citizens – you better Wake up and do it!

However the nation ultimately decides to rationalize its chaotic and incoherent immigration system, surely all can agree that, at a minimum, authorities should expel illegal-alien criminals swiftly. Even on the grounds of protecting non-criminal illegal immigrants, we should start by junking sanctuary policies. By stripping cops of what may be their only immediate tool to remove felons from the community, these policies leave law-abiding immigrants prey to crime.

But the non-enforcement of immigration laws in general has an even more destructive effect. In many immigrant communities, assimilation into gangs seems to be outstripping assimilation into civic culture. Toddlers are learning to flash gang signals and hate the police, reports the Los Angeles Times. In New York City, "every high school has its Mexican gang," and most 12- to 14-year-olds have already joined, claims Ernesto Vega, an illegal 18-year-old

Mexican. Such pathologies only worsen when the first lesson that immigrants learn about U.S. law is that Americans don't bother to enforce it. "Institutionalizing illegal immigration creates a mindset in people that anything goes in the U.S.," observes Patrick Ortega, the news and public-affairs director of Radio Nueva Vida in southern California. "It creates a new subculture, with a sequela of social ills." It is broken windows written in large letters.

For the sake of immigrants and native-born Americans alike, it's time to decide what our immigration policy is—and enforce it or kiss America goodby."

The following disgusting tirade and pure and plain sedition plans to destroy America through violence could not be presented in a more arrogant and definitive manner and represents statements of several Mexican hate groups planning to overthrow the American Government.

What is our government agencies doing about this deadly threat to America's security? ABSOLUTELY NOTHING! Rumors have it that orders are coming down from the White House to leave these groups alone to continue to threaten and Gang murder American citizens while they complete plans to take over one town or city at a time as the police stand and watch. It is pathetic to watch the paralysis and crumbling of American society caused by one individual who lied to the American people when being sworn in to the office of President of the United States of America! Here's his sworn oath, you be the judge:

I,_A,B_, do solemnly swear or (affirm) that I will support and defend the Constitution of the United States against all enemies, foreign and domestic, that I will bear true faith and allegiance to the same, that I take this obligation freely, without any mental reservation or purpose of evasion; and that I will well and faithfully discharge the office of which I am about to enter

So Help Me God!

Is the United States being protected from enemies – Answer NO! – America is being swamped by declared enemies and nothing is done. The American people, placing their confidence and trust in those elected to guide our nation forward with continued prosperity, safety and security, have instead been betrayed by conspiracy, deceit and closed session secrecy to reduce America to a giant garbage dump, the stench and smell of which will pervade and prevail for generations as has the country of origin – Mexico! The courage, intelligence, and dedication to being honorable, honest and trustworthy human beings which was a hallmark of our nation's founders, is not present in our government today, which is without doubt the most corrupt, dishonest, self-gratifying and low down collection of traitors ever accumulated in one bunch, at one time, in the history of the United States – top to bottom!

To demonstrate the disparity of the present government loyalty to America versus the hordes of criminals invading the United States, if the statements below were made by an American group to the acknowledged Mexican criminals, one hour would not pass until the FBI, CIA, and so-called Home Security bunch would be slapping handcuffs on Real Americans for plotting against America! This is America?

No! This is what the American people are facing today with a government showing every indication of embracing Mexican takeover with 150 Million leaving Mexico and dropping babies all over America – half illegitimate. This is the future of America in the next twenty years.   Thank you Mr. Bush!

"You (gringos) have spilled enough of our blood, now it's your turn to bleed, you sub-human beasts." So said an editorial in the University of California Irvine's Hispanic LaVoz Mestiza. Professor Gutierrez, employed by the University of Texas, founder of La Raza said, "We have got to eliminate the gringo, and what I mean by that is if the worst comes to the worst, we have got to kill him."

Please read carefully the information presented at the close of this book (so it will stick in your mind) for full disclosure of several Mexican outlaw organizations formation and purpose brazenly disclosed and the lousy government officials too scared and yellow to order law enforcement to arrest and deport the garbage!

A Chicano hate organization called MEChA wants to take over much of the US Southwest, an area they call Aztlan said, "For the race everything. For those outside the race, nothing." Other similar hate groups include: The La Raza Unida Party, Brown Berets de Aztlan, OLA (Organization for the Liberation of Aztlan), and the Nation of Aztlan. These are radical organizations that can be found in many American high schools and most colleges. They hate America and love its enemies. They are brimming over with race hatred, anti-Semitism, and a history of communist leanings and communist support. They have an irrational anger aimed at their stupid benefactors. Recent mass marches have emboldened these people who do pose a real threat to this nation. Many are illegals and profess their allegiance not to the United States where they live, but to the authoritarian corrupt state of Mexico.

Why are these Chicano groups willing to use violence, kill the gringo, and steal his home and land? : "There are some Mexican citizens and some Mexican -Americans who want to see California, New Mexico and other parts of the southwestern United States given over to Mexico. These groups call it the reconquista, Spanish for reconquest."

MEChA has declared war on the United States, the Constitution, and the Declaration of Independence. So far it has done this with impunity with the help of treacherous senators, congressmen, university officials, along with other enemies of this nation. MEChA is bold and aggressive using this nation's economy, welfare programs, its educational system and cooperation of low down cowardly officials. (What is your opinion Arnold?) While filling their bellies and needs at the expense of the American taxpayer, they're plotting the overthrow of this republic in broad daylight. MEChA is nurtured and protected by the University of California (Traitorous SOB's) at Irvine. MEChA has spread its venomous rhetoric through an estimated 300 chapters in universities and schools across the United States. Their plan EL PLAN DE AZTLÁN is available for all to read. It's full of race hated, threats, and the use of their bodies for war and their youth to commit revolutionary acts of violence against this nation and its people.

George Bush has betrayed our nation by deliberately assisting the illegal immigrants to swamp America and continuing to lie to the American people. Mr. Bush's intentions toward America have a lot of suspicious overtones and there are many disturbed people calling for his impeachment. There can be no excuse for abetting the hordes of immigrants swamping America –none! See Oath of Office!

MEChA is appealing to all Hispanics to join their so- called revolution. The illegal aliens and lack of national border control are issues that are developing into a life or death struggle determining whether this republic shall endure as we have know it for the past 230 years. This is a threat with a potential that rivals Iran and radical Islam and it's in our communities and cities across the nation. Our national leaders are turning their backs to this threat while smiling and looking for Hispanic votes. (Stupid Traitorous SOB's). The illegal aliens are the grunts for an army of gorilla fighters MEChA and other Chicano groups would like to create. Amnesty will make no difference to them, for the beat of their drums will continue. With amnesty, millions more of Mexico's poor and hungry will attempt to enter the US for a free ride on the backs of US taxpayers until the nation collapses and dies!

There are large numbers of Hispanics who will never integrate into this society. They are not learning English as shown by the number of Spanish radio stations, businesses that tell you to push one for Spanish or two for English, and bilingual schools. Whole communities, like Maywood, California, in Los Angeles are nearly 100 percent Hispanic. And their allegiance to a lousy corrupt Mexico, though hard to understand, is obvious. – they're stupid! This was demonstrated visually when Hispanics legal and illegals filled American streets with protestors wanting open boarders, and amnesty for illegals, while waving Mexican flags. There was a backlash to the Mexican flag waving, so now they wave American flags thinking to fool the watchers, thus making them hypocrites and liars.

Demonstrations like this don't happen in Mexico where Mexican authorities rape, rob, and beat illegals passing through their territory.

Mexico supports illegal aliens leaving Mexico and illegally crossing our border but doesn't want illegals coming in.

MEChA says in the Plan, "A nation autonomous and free - culturally, socially, economically, and politically- will make its own decisions on the usage of our lands, the taxation of our goods, the utilization of our bodies for war, the determination of justice (reward and punishment), and the profit of our sweat." The, "our lands" is the land owned by American citizens. How does MEChA propose to obtain this land of the southwestern states? Their Plan indicates they will use violence with physical force to remove the gringo from his property. Let's look at the following statements from the Plan.

> " Education must be relative to our people, i.e., history, culture, bilingual education, contributions, etc. Community control of our schools, our teachers, our administrators, our counselors, and our programs."

> "POLITICAL LIBERATION can only come through independent action on our part, since the two-party system is the same animal with two heads that feed from the same trough. Where we are a majority, we will control; where we are a minority, we will represent a pressure group; nationally, we will represent one party: La Familia de La Raza!"

> "El Plan de Aztlán is the plan of liberation! Those institutions which are fattened by our brothers to provide employment and political pork barrels for the gringo will do so only as acts of liberation and for La Causa. For the very young there will no longer be acts of juvenile delinquency, but revolutionary acts."

> "We must insure that our writers, poets, musicians, and artists produce literature and art that is appealing to our people and relates to our revolutionary culture."

One could reasonably ask why MEChA doesn't make Mexico an economic powerhouse. The answer is easy; they are having so much success in the US, and they want to steal, like thieves in the night, the wealth of someone else's hard work. The goose that lays the golden egg is in mortal danger from the blind men in our government.

California taxpayers paid an extra nine billion dollars to support illegals according to a 2004 report by the Federation for American Immigration Reform, a Washington, D.C. organization that endorses stricter immigration policies. Contributing to this expense are education at around $8 thousand per illegal child or those born to illegal parents, medical care, and prison costs. A similar study in 2004 by the Center for Immigration Studies in Washington, D.C. claimed that illegal aliens cost the federal government $10 billion more than is collected in taxes from them.

That includes $2.2 billion for medical care for uninsured illegal aliens. Another $1.9 billion goes to food assistance programs like food stamps and school lunch programs. Illegal immigrant children cost taxpayers $1.4 billion in aid to schools to help pay their costs. The states' taxpayers carry the major part of the cost to care for the millions of illegals in this country. When schools ask for more money, ask how many illegals are in the classroom and if the citizenship of the parents and child was checked. The costs mentioned are disputed by others who claim the costs of illegals aliens is much higher.

Illegals are creating a huge crime wave all across the United States. Here is what Russell Pearce, representing Arizona's 18th district says on his website, "Perhaps as high as 80% of the violent crime in the Phoenix area involves illegal aliens (according to Phoenix Chief Hurt and Mesa police violent crimes response team). Over 4000 homicide warrants were issued by the Border States to suspects who are believed to have fled south of the border into Mexico. Maricopa County Hospital loses over $2 million weekly on uncompensated care (largely do to illegal aliens). In 2003, 77 border hospitals filed for bankruptcy."

The US is a big candy land for the uneducated, criminals, and often sick illegal aliens. The illegals aliens have found there is a free lunch, free medical care, free education, and there really is a Santos Claus, a big, stupid, pale-faced gringo. Hispanic Professor Jose Angel Gutierrez at the University of Texas describes the gringo as, "Our

Devil with pale skin and blue eyes." This pale-faced gringo sounds more like a fool than a devil. And guess who the all day sucker is; it's none other than John Q. Taxpayer. He's represented in congress by a bunch of enablers called congressmen and senators including Sen. John McCain and company. Jack Abramoff isn't the only guy that should be behind bars.

That America's two most recent presidents, Bill Clinton and George W. Bush, have been guilty of intentionally flawed and fallacious decisions and activities is obvious. However, at what point do bad policies and conduct become treasonous? At what point do we conclude that our country's Chief Executive has crossed the line of mere inanity or naïveté and has actually become a threat to our national security and survival?

There is a plethora of evidence to support the accusation that then-President Bill Clinton deliberately facilitated the transfer of military (including rocket and satellite) technology to Communist China in exchange for large donations via highly placed Chinese operatives. That, more than the Monica Lewinsky affair, should have been the basis of impeachment. However, the Republican majority in Congress chose to do absolutely nothing about Clinton's treasonous conduct in Chinagate. Now it is President George W. Bush who is pushing the envelope.

As I have already stated in this column, I believe an independent investigation should proceed aggressively in order to determine whether or not President Bush and Vice President Dick Cheney deliberately manufactured evidence to support a preemptive invasion of Iraq. If it is proven they did, they should both be impeached.

However, I believe there is another area of malfeasance committed by G.W. Bush that is equal to anything Bill Clinton did: his determination to facilitate a Mexican invasion of the United States and the decision to merge America into a trilateral North American Community.

It is no hyperbole to say that Bush's infatuation with Mexican immigration and uniting the economy of the U.S. with those of

Canada and Mexico threatens the sovereignty and independence of our country, not to mention our national security.

One former military analyst is quoted as saying, "We are under attack. Twenty million have already entered the country, and more are to come. And sadly, many of our leaders are siding with the invaders. They are willing to spend billions of dollars to deport foreigners from Iraq and defend Iraq's borders, but won't lift a finger to save the USA."

William Calhoun wrote, "We know that Hispanics in the Mexican military are helping Arab terrorists sneak into the United States. We know that many Mexican gangs have already made alliances with terrorist cells in India."

Calhoun continued by saying, "In short, Hispanics plan to retake the Southwest United States. Reconquista, is what they call it, and their aim is for Aztlan to live once again. As Mexican activist Ricky Sierra said, 'We are recolonizing America . . . .. It is time for us to take back what is ours.'"

Not only has President Bush turned a blind eye to the gigantic national security risks posed by unfettered illegal immigration, he has become the most outspoken expeditor of illegal immigration.

For example, just recently, President Bush gave a directive to the Texas Court of Criminal Appeals demanding that a convicted Mexican rapist and murderer on death row be given another hearing. In what is obviously an attempt to grovel before and appease the Mexican government, Bush used an International Court of Justice ruling to justify this presidential intrusion into the State of Texas's judicial affairs.

The murderer's name is Jose Ernesto Medellin. He was one of six gang members convicted of brutally raping and killing two Houston teenagers Jennifer Ertman and Elizabeth Pena, who stumbled upon a violent gang initiation. But George W. Bush wants him taken off death row and given another hearing.

Thankfully, the Texas Court of Criminal Appeals has no intention of being bullied by this rogue president. Judge Michael Keasler wrote that Bush "exceeded his constitutional authority by intruding into the independent powers of the judiciary." Presiding Judge Sharon Keller said that Bush's "unprecedented, unnecessary, and intrusive exercise of power over the Texas court system cannot be supported by the foreign policy authority conferred on him by the United States Constitution." (Source: The Fort Worth Star-Telegram)

Remember, this is the same president that, at the behest of the Mexican government, turned the U.S. Attorney's office loose on two U.S. Border Patrol agents and a Texas Deputy Sheriff. According to Jerome Corsi, "Investigators had no plans to bring charges against Texas Sheriff's Deputy Gilmer Hernandez until the Mexican government intervened and demanded it.

"Sheriff Don Letsinger of Rocksprings, Texas, said the Texas Rangers were not going to recommend prosecution, but federal law enforcement took over the case in response to the Mexican government's intervention."

I trust that readers are also aware that in continuing to accommodate illegal immigration and placate the Mexican government that promotes it, President Bush is ignoring the fact that, according to Congressman Steve King (R-Iowa), illegal aliens murder twelve Americans each day. That equates to more Americans being killed by illegal aliens each year than have been killed in Iraq and Afghanistan to date.

Now we hear that "the Bush administration is fully committed to beginning within weeks a pilot test that will allow Mexican trucks to operate freely across the U.S." Think of the thousands of U.S. workers that will ultimately be displaced by Bush's decision to launch Mexican trucks all across America. Not to mention the potential safety and security problems that will ensue.

The question is again: At what point do bad policies and conduct become treasonous? At what point do we conclude that our country's Chief Executive has crossed the line of mere insanity or naïveté and

115

has actually become a threat to our national security and survival? It is believed Bill Clinton crossed that line and also George W. Bush has crossed that line.

The problem is, hardly anyone in Washington, D.C., has the guts to do anything about it. For one thing, many of our congressmen and senators from both major parties are equally culpable in both Clinton's and Bush's chicanery. They are yellow belly old fat men, crooks and traitors!

Let's face it, Real Americans: we are living under a government saturated with corruption. It's time we admitted it. No! It's time we did something about it. I hope and pray that that, regardless of whether Republicans or Democrats control it, is the American people will wake up and realize that they have the authority and power to throw off this bunch of scoundrels. It's called the ballot box, and we need to use it to thoroughly clean house. And we need to do it while we still can.

As Winston Churchill said, "If you will not fight for the right when you can easily win without bloodshed, if you will not fight when your victory will be sure and not so costly, you may come to the moment when you will have to fight with all the odds against you and only a precarious chance for survival. There may be a worse case. You may have to fight even when it looks as there is no hope of victory, because it is better to perish than to live as slaves."

It is important to recognize that the once puzzling attitude of George Bush in ignoring the swamping of America by Hispanic Illegal Immigrants is now obvious. The information has been made public recently that George Bush has been actively working behind the people of America's back to establish the North American Union (NAU) which will include Canada, the United States and MEXICO! This statement is verified by the complete and total absence of any public announcement and information to the American citizens. It is they who will be the victims of such a dastardly and underhanded slap in the face! America is being attacked with a two edged sword – 1. Deliberately instigated planned "open border" illegal immigration and 2.The Trilateral Deception of the North American Union, each one designed to draw attention from the other until America has been destroyed. America deserves an explanation from Mr. Bush but will never hear it –until the day he says –GOTCHA! – unless Real Americans wake up and shove these plans you know where ! It is the duty of our Senators and Congressmen to pass legislation to make such disloyal acts an impeachment offense! If this unholy trilateral alliance is allowed to bear fruition, citizens of America can kiss this nation goodbye. This is the beginning of One World Order which has been in concept for years by the so-called "elite super humans" who are in reality nothing more than power hungry traitors to their respective countries. Betraying the trust placed in them by loyal citizens is committing treason and calls for impeachment. Can the connection now be made between Illegal Immigration open borders and the NAU? Yes!

It is important to first understand that the impending birth of the NAU is the baby and brainstorm of the Executive Branch of the U.S. government, - namely, G. Bush and cohorts - not the Congress. The U.S. Congress should immediately pass a measure to prevent the President of the United States from privately negotiating treaties suiting his desires. This is blatantly obvious when observing the activities of G. Bush. If a preventive controlling measure had been in place earlier, the traitorous NAFTA agreement would have been shoved up the respective you know what of Bill Clinton, Henry Kissinger and other "Big Shot" traitors. It is unbelievable that America and her people can be betrayed with so many underhanded back stabbing methods by those who have the idea they are the intelligentsia and everybody else is a dumb slob.

THE LOW DOWN DIRT

"THE GLOBAL THEORY OF FREE trade is siphoning off America's wealth and bringing her economy to the level of others. The theory is displacing American workers who otherwise would be employed." Senator George Malone, 1958

First plank of the communist manifesto: abolition of all private property. Eminent domain is sweeping this country like a deadly forest fire and it will continue to escalate as plans for the complete and total destruction of our sovereign nation move ahead. Bush's proposed North American Union (NAU) and the so-called Security and Prosperity Partnership of North America (SPP) are the final nails in the coffin of America's sovereignty. The globalists in Congress and the White House over the past several decades have been slowly, step by step deconstructing our sovereign republic in anticipation of eliminating these United States of America and merging them into one region of a world governmental body. Congressman Ron Paul summed it up this way:

"By now many Texans have heard about the proposed "NAFTA Superhighway," which is also referred to as the trans-Texas corridor. What you may not know is the extent to which plans for such a superhighway are moving forward without congressional oversight or media attention."

Printed by Permission

By Devvy Kidd, Journalist & Lecturer:

This superhighway would connect Mexico, the United States, and Canada, cutting a wide swath through the middle of Texas and up through Kansas City. Offshoots would connect the main artery to the west coast, Florida, and northeast. Proponents envision a ten-lane colossus the width of several football fields, with freight and rail lines, fiber-optic cable lines, and oil and natural gas pipelines running alongside.

This will require coordinated federal and state eminent domain actions on an unprecedented scale, as literally millions of people and businesses could be displaced. The loss of whole communities is almost certain, as planners cannot wind the highway around every quaint town, historic building, or senior citizen apartment for thousands of miles.

"The SPP was first launched in 2005 by the heads of state of Canada, Mexico, and the United States at a summit in Waco. The SPP was not created by a treaty between the nations involved, nor was Congress involved in any way. Instead, the SPP is an unholy alliance of foreign consortiums and officials from several governments. One principal player is a Spanish construction company, which plans to build the highway and operate it as a toll road. But don't be fooled: the superhighway proposal is not the result of free market demand, but rather an extension of government-managed trade schemes like NAFTA that benefit politically-connected interests.

The real issue is national sovereignty. Once again, decisions that affect millions of Americans are not being made by those Americans themselves, or even by their elected representatives in Congress. Instead, a handful of elites use their government connections to bypass national legislatures and ignore our Constitution – which expressly grants Congress the sole authority to regulate international trade.

The ultimate goal is not simply a superhighway, but an integrated North American Union – complete with a currency, a cross-national bureaucracy, and virtually borderless travel within the Union. Like the European Union, a North American Union would represent another step toward the abolition of national sovereignty altogether.

In July 2006, I traveled to Austin, Texas to take a look at this trans-Texas corridor. It is a monstrous construction feat that has been years in the making right under everyone's nose until Phyllis Schlafly and then Jerome Corsi, began exposing this insidious plan. There is a four minute video cartoon on how Gov. Rick Perry (Texas) has sold out the sovereignty of our republic for big money. While this is a cartoon, it is 100% factual. This is top priority national issue. Watch it. Get it. This NAU is going to get you in one way or another if it isn't stopped. Thousands of businesses, ranches, farms and homes will be seized under eminent domain (a 4,000 miles long gutting) to complete this sell out of America. Perry allegedly won reelection a couple of weeks ago. That's what electronic machines are for: making sure those individuals who have proven their loyalty to their global masters remain in office so the agenda goes forward. Texans need to resurrect, "Remember the Alamo" and soon because the eminent domain sledgehammer will crank up next year and then watch the carnage.

119

While in Austin, I did my usual questioning of everyone from hotel employees to retail clerks and restaurant workers. The response was all the same: this trans-corridor was a God-send because it brought jobs and billions of dollars into the area. Oh, boy, it's going to cut down on traffic problems! and that's how it's been sold as a "Texas Department of Transportation initiative proposed to solve critical transportation problems in the State of Texas." Horse feathers. Not a single person I questioned had any idea of what it really means for our republic and I doubt much they would care because jobs are the name of the game.

This is how the destroyers have the people by the throat. NAFTA and GATT have destroyed our most important job bases: agriculture, manufacturing and industrial. Out of work Americans were run off their land, out of the factories and into huge, crime infested metropolitan cities totally unprepared causing their infrastructures and legal systems to near breaking point. Now it's anything to keep your head above water as more as more Americans slide into poverty. The middle class is being killed off and a new peonage system will develop in what used to be America if this NAU succeeds. Lord, our Founding Fathers must wonder why they and all the thousands whose blood ran in rivers to give us a free republic even bothered.

As Ron Paul says above, there will be a new currency because there has to be. While many Americans would rather hide their head in the sand, the financial picture is an ugly one. America's debt is not sustainable and the worst is coming. A couple of weeks ago I had a very long phone conversation with Dr. Edwin Vieira about this very subject and the timing of this trans-corridor/North American Union, the manipulation of the stock market as the "FED" tries to keep it propped up and a two tiered monetary system. I asked Edwin to write a column on this and hopefully he will soon. Unless and until the American people understand the money mechanics, they won't be able to comprehend what's coming that will affect them and their family.

Millions of Americans simply haven't been able to understand why Bush has refused to close the borders or make any attempt whatsoever to stop the massive invasion of illegals. As soon as the veil was lifted on this North American Union and the Security and Prosperity Partnership of North America, it all made sense even to his most loyal supporters. Bush has never had any intention of upholding the laws of this land because his job is to cement the final pieces of one world government along with bankrupting US with his endless, unconstitutional "wars of liberation."

Why do you think this voluntary National ID card surfaced and is scheduled for 2008? Because Bush and his global masters intend for the destruction of our republic to be complete by 2010. Do Americans really understand what this means? All the blood that has been shed to keep America a free nation will have been spilled for nothing. It means the death of our nation, our constitution, our Bill of Rights. It means inheriting another 100 million illiterate poor from Mexico, making all of US "global citizens" in this nightmare scheme. Years ago I wrote about grade school children in Red Bluff, California being given textbook lessons on becoming a global citizen. No American history, just pure propaganda. Forward planning and it's been underway for decades while Americans walk around in their self imposed comas or fighting at retail stores for the latest junk from commie China: a Sony play station. Adults fighting over a toy while Bush burns the U.S. Constitution and Bill of Rights. Think about that and this:

"The open plan to merge the US with Mexico and Canada and create a Pan American Union networked by a NAFTA Super Highway has long been a Globalist brainchild but its very real and prescient implementation on behalf of the Council on Foreign Relations has recently come under bright spotlight. According to author Jerome Corsi, "Across the NAFTA Super-Highways will flow millions more Mexicans, now armed with North American border passes and biometric identification, as defined by the Security and Prosperity Partnership of North America working groups organized within the Department of Commerce."

The Council on Foreign Relations is an evil operation, a subject I have written about extensively over the past decade plus. These people are our enemy and you should know their faces; see here and this one courtesy of an American who cares; this list was obtained from the Seeley Mudd library at Princeton University. The American Empire: Conquest Through NAFTA is another in depth look at the connection between the destruction of our sovereign country and the CFR.

In August 2006, I traveled to Laredo, Texas to interview a U.S. Border Patrol agent who is retiring. While there I saw the huge construction underway of another section of the trans-Texas corridor.

My new friend drove me all around town and gave me a very good history lesson on illegals smuggling themselves across the border, the hot spots and the drug corridors. As I stood on the bank of the Rio Grande and looked across at Mexico, the international bridge joining the two countries was packed like sardines; a human wave. Day workers, visitors and illegals trying to get through with forged documents. On the USA side of the Rio Grande, the first ten blocks going North looks just like the slums of Mexico and like the LA basin, it will come to your town. One or two businesses are in English, but the rest is all Spanish and having been to Tijuana and the interior of Mexico, I know what I've seen and to see it being birthed in America is tragic.

Any Texas State legislator who voted for House Bill 3588 back in 2003 which amended the Texas Transportation code to give the state the broad, new powers needed to build the Trans-Texas Corridor should have been thrown out of office two weeks ago. Now they should be the target of all Texas groups fighting to stop this move to destroy our republic the next time they're up for reelection. It is simply beyond words that elected officials, governors, state legislators and members of Congress are allowing America to be sold off to foreign interests and governments. It is an outrage and it is killing US. Texans need to begin bombarding their state legislators to stop this NAU and the SPP by telling Washington, DC we will not give up our sovereignty. I know this will be difficult since most of them are bought and paid for by big business in this state, but if hundreds of thousands of Texans make their voices good and loud, the roar of the lion hearted will scare the mice.

We are in the fight for our very existence and no one should doubt it for a second. This is it and every single American must step up to the plate and do their part. Yes, we have several other crucial wars going on, i.e., stopping the upcoming amnesty sell out by the Democrats with assistance from some traitorous Republicans which will be kissed by Bush and getting rid of draconian and unconstitutional junk laws like the John Warner Defense Authorization Act. These treasonous mechanisms are all inter-related and we must attack all of them as our top priorities until we run these globalists out of America and return to an independent, self sustaining nation.

How? First thing in January: Bombard Congress to adopt H. Con. Res. 487 or a new bill with the same text except change this: "Expressing the sense of Congress that the United States should not engage in the construction of a North American Free Trade Agreement (NAFTA) Superhighway System or enter into a North... (Introduced in House)." There is no expression or sense about this. Change it to "These united States of America will not enter into or engage in the construction of a North American Free Trade Agreement (NAFTA) Superhighway System or enter into a North... (Introduced in House)." Concurrently, we must get at least one state legislature to force a showdown on the Seventeenth Amendment; see here to understand why.

Once this legislation is passed, Bush must sign it and if he refuses, Congress can over ride his treachery. Second: Stop the Security and Prosperity Partnership. Stop SPP is a project of MinutemenProject. com. Get involved now because it's the eleventh hour. Get creative. Paint a big sign and put it in your front yard: 'Stop the merging of US with Canada and Mexico' Your neighbors will want to know what it's all about. Put the StopSPP web site address below the headline so people reading your sign will have someplace to go to find out what this means. Don't put this off. Advertising pays and we need to bring this to the attention of all of our fellow Americans from Vermont to San Diego, Tampa to Anchorage. There's no longer any pursuit of happiness, just the war we're fighting for our freedom and sovereignty and this means sacrifice by all of us, not just a few.

Get very public which means going down to your local VFW or other organizations in your city or town and make this issue the number one dialogue. Tragically, we lost the Panama Canal to the communist Chinese because the American people were too busy. The commies are now lining up at the Texas ports in anticipation of this NAU and I cannot emphasize strongly enough that the communist Chinese are our enemy, not our friend. Please stop supporting communism with your hard earned money; buy Made in the USA. It's easy and it's the right thing to do for America. Stop supporting slave labor used by the communist Chinese government. More than 58,000 Americans died in the jungles of Viet Nam to stop the proliferation of communism, yet Americans continue to enrich the coffers of communist regimes. Stupid public officials let the first flood gates open in Long Beach, California and the commies got their foot in the door big time. Don't let the same thing happen with this NAU and the SPP.

The Mexican government has deliberately treated its people as little better than cattle, and for the past decade, the drug lords have come in and are Columbia-izing Mexico. This horrific situation will simply be imported into our country on a mass scale if this NAU and the SPP isn't stopped, period. Get to your political party meetings, attend city council meetings, board of supervisor meetings and start talking about this. Take a nice flyer with you that has the Stop SPP web site information. There's no one else to do this, but each of us in our counties. It won't be the mind numbing Shawn Hannity or the LA Times telling the American people the truth, it has to be you and me. We must begin to bury Congress with our demands that this whole process be shut down.

It's too late to stop some construction of the roads, but we can and must stop this from going further before our fellow Americans are thrown off their land via eminent domain. All the agreements must be nullified, our sovereignty protected, the border closed and the fence built across the border with Mexico. This is our country, not Rick Perry's, not some company out of Spain and not George Bush's. Our children and grand children deserve their birthright to be free in a free united States of America. I pray Americans won't be too busy to do their part because that's exactly what the destroyers are counting on: laziness and apathy.

I will NOT live under international laws. I will NOT surrender my Second Amendment rights for any world body and that's just the way it's going to be. Land of the free, home of the brave? We shall see.

Bush Lacks Common Sense That God Gave A Goose By Frosty Wooldridge

4-17-7

Reprinted by permission:

While we kids grew up, my father often said,

"Use your common sense before you make decisions."

At other times, when he saw someone reaching under a running power-mower to clear the grass, or pitching a baseball with a kid standing in front of a plate glass window, he lamented,

"Those guys don't have the common sense

God gave a goose!"

Today, my late father, a 27-year master sergeant in the United States Marine Corps, would certainly shake his head in disbelief after hearing the latest speech from President George W. Bush, by saying,

"That guy doesn't have an ounce of common sense."

He would say the same about the Pelosi-Reid-Kennedy troika, and the equally foolish Flake-Gutierrez duo. We have captive idiots at the helm today.

What is common sense?

According to the dictionary, "Sound and prudent judgment."

After terrorists bombed America out of its perceived safety on 9/11, common sense dictated that we take energetic steps to totally control our borders and STOP immigrating into our country people from terrorist regions around the world.

Additionally, common sense mandated that we FIRST secure our leakiest southern borders from terrorist incursions.

Instead, Bush led attacks on Iraq- 10,000 miles away- while leaving our continental U.S. borders wide open. In his open-borders mania, he continues immigrating millions of people from the land of Islam- as if none of them might become terrorists on our own soil.

Please, help me here; Can anyone figure out what Bush uses for common sense ?

Iraq-Afghanistan Study Group; Hon. James Baker

After the James Baker's Iraq Study Group showed the United States couldn't win Iraq's civil war, common sense dictated that Bush best begin logical, prudent and rational withdrawal from an un-winnable and deadly conflict.

Even if we won that war, what would we win?

Instead of withdrawing, Bush sent in more soldiers that, as the news illustrates every week, die or suffer horrific amputations along with other misery in an unending spiral of violence.

I must concede that there have been mini-successes, but- at what price ?

Meanwhile- What's happening on "the mainland?"

All the while, a documented 13 million American children live below the poverty line, and another 1.3 million American children suffer homelessness. Many do not have enough to eat, and get precious little in medical and social-services care.

A whopping 14 million unemployed Americans struggle with joblessness, hopelessness and uselessness- depression is rampant. Due to a "cutsy" approach to counting heads, the Bureau of Labor (BLS) does not count the 20 million more- the "chronically unemployed."

Meanwhile, Bush rebuilds Iraq's society with American taxpayer dollars. Correction: he's spent $789 billion on credit to be paid by future generations. Next year at this time, the invoice will surpass a TRILLION U.S. dollars !

If you're not angry, you're part of the problem

Our president does nothing to change the status of 14 million unemployed Americans, the 20 million "chronically employed," our 3.3 million homeless adults (many Vietnam vets) and our 1.3 million homeless children.

What are we thinking ?

Meanwhile, he allowed more than ten million legal immigrants to flood America in the first six years of his administration- many being people that further erode jobs, housing and schools for American families.

At the same time, an estimated 20 million illegal aliens crossed our borders without inspection, while Bush makes excuses for them to be here illegally-and wants to grant them amnesty. Do bank-robbers get amnesty ?

Where is the common sense ?

The illusion of progress

Last month, Bush told Americans that this country would drop oil consumption by 20 percent in ten years by 2017. How?

"We'll promote ethanol, hybrid cars and conservation."

What didn't he tell the public? In the same 10 years, America will increase its population by 30 million people, or more, thus negating any conservation. This population increase will be far worse if the Kennedy-Pelosi-Reid team gets the amnesty and guest-workers that our president covets.

The 1986-IRCA amnesty circus taught us- stupid is as stupid does. The 3.4 million granted amnesty and citizenship back then have resulted in nearly 40 million more citizens today- by having babies and sponsoring more naturalized citizens. Inevitable.

Pollution increases tell the story

The process proves simple- adding that many people increases consumption. Where is the common sense? That increases things like greenhouse gases, water pollution, etc.

Even more sobering: how could the American people remain so naïve, or perhaps a better word- stupid , to accept the incompetence of Congress and Bush ?

Trade-deficits and jobs lost

In the past six years of the Bush administration, annual trade deficits run $700 billion- almost exactly what the Iraq-Afghanistan wars cost YOU, the American taxpayers. Double trouble !

We are sitting like lemmings- while foreign-nationals eat our proverbial lunch.

During the recent six years -- over three million manufacturing jobs vacated our country. More than one million American IT jobs were swallowed up by foreign-nationals here with H-1B, H-2B and L-1 visas.

Dumb and dumber.

We have "forgotten" how to compete and manage successfully

Chrysler, owned by a powerful German multi-national conglomerate, is failing and is now for sale. General Motors and Ford dangle at the end of their collective hooks like so many steer carcasses in a packing plant- as they drop 30,000 jobs in two years. Meanwhile, the high-integrity Toyota builds more and more U.S. factories.

All of these failures are easily traced to our lack of sensible strategic plans.

Where, for instance, is our U.S. National Immigration Strategic Plan ? Would you be surprised to learn- there is nobody singularly in charge of immigration in the U.S. Instead, we have tactical bureaucratic geniuses in fiefdoms competing with one-another, dancing to the tune of the U.S. Chamber of Commerce- Departments of State, Labor, Commerce, DHS, and others. Incredibly stupid!

As my father would say, "Why doesn't Bush use common sense?"

Expensive social-services for illegal aliens come first.

While 40 million Americans can't afford health insurance for themselves and their children, Bush supports more than 20 million illegal aliens and their children & grand-children with automatic "free" health care in every hospital in this country.

He supports more than 380,000 illegal alien mothers birthing 380,000 anchor babies annually with full funding from American taxpayers. Average birth, pre-natal and post-natal care cost no less than $8,000 to $12,000 per kid, depending on region of the country. If such a child suffers premature birth or birth defect, costs run into the millions.

While our deficit president supports illegal aliens abusing our rights, he won't support American citizens and their children with basic health care. Where is the common sense of that ?

Foreclosures are the tip of the iceberg

With home foreclosures reaching epidemic levels, consumer debt at $2 trillion and the average credit card holder suffering a $9,149.00 balance- wouldn't it, and please follow me here, wouldn't it make common sense that President Bush, for once, represent American workers, American interests, American children, America education and our culture?

Instead of blowing off $2 billion a week paying for the Iraq-Afghanistan Wars- based on the threat of illusionary WMD (weapons of mass destruction), better known as "Willful Mass Deception," wouldn't it make more sense to exert a stop-loss effort; bring our troops home, stop the killing-maiming, guard our own borders and perhaps spend money on America's interests, i.e., our own children and citizens?

Wouldn't it make more common sense for Bush to deal with and resolve America and America's challenges? Wouldn't it make more sense to guard our borders from terrorists instead of provoking more terrorism in the land of Islam?

Finally, the worst nightmare Bush bequeaths upon future Americans finds his dirty little secret of jumping legal immigration from 1 to 2 million annually. His actions today propel us toward an added 100 million people by 2040. If we don't have enough problems today with air pollution, gridlocked cities, crowding, endangered species, climate change, educational, medical and other problems, Bush adds to our social nightmare by jumping our population issues from insane to ultra insane. In other words, Bush has taken leave of his senses as he forces us down his insane path.

We suffer from a leadership mess

The U.S. Congress cowers in the pocket of the U.S. Chamber of Commerce- puppets to big-business and their dirty racketeering. The 'checks-and-balances' are smoke-and-mirrors- illusion. Our forefathers roll in their graves.

Bush proves daily a man out of his league. He possesses no vision, shows no direction or understanding of the dilemma he forces on America. He uses no reasoned approach to our nation's pressing challenges. Instead, he reaps dishonor upon this fragile Republic, chaos in Iraq and misery upon our citizens.

The "silliest" one yet- President Bush cleverly sent the best and brightest of the DHS C&BP (Border Patrol) to secure the Iraq borders, while our borders remain wide-open, and our Border Patrol is short 80,000 officers.

How else can the illicit drugs from Mexico come here to induce our people into a stupor?

As my father Master Sergeant Howard Wooldridge would say, "President George W. Bush lacks the common sense that God gave a goose!"

ENGRAVED ON AMERICA'S TOMBSTONE?

By Frosty Wooldridge

Reprinted by permission

In 476 AD, Rome vanished into the history books. It was a heck of a run: Rome began as a Republic; it conquered most of the known world; it became an empire; it enjoyed slavery; it built lavish architecture still admired into the 21st century; Rome constructed the Coliseum where one million men suffered slaughtering in 200 years of the 'games'; it partied with decadence in wine, women and song; Mark Anthony and Cleopatra's passions became the stuff of legends; finally, Julius Caesar took knives in his gut; et tu Brutus?

You've read Rome's demise in history books. Shakespeare immortalized great moments. You've seen the movies with Charlton Heston, Yul Brenner and Elizabeth Taylor. Rome's greatness stretched for centuries, but it declined to its grave on the Boot Hill of history.

We see the similarities of Rome manifesting in America in the early years of the 21st century. Republic to empire; military bases in 100 countries around the world; Donald Trump nauseates us with his skyscrapers; 100,000 seat NFL stadiums entertaining the masses with outrageous salaried 'gladiators' and booze; Brad and Angelina's endless nothingness; young men dying without reason in the contrived Iraq war; et tu Bushtus?

What will be engraved on America's tombstone if it doesn't stop an endless immigrant invasion? Who will write the words? Why did it happen? Who aided it within America's borders? Will they be brought to justice? Why did they do it to their own country? To their own children? To the future?

A noble citizen wrote me last week with quotes from the late Ayn Rand, "Which of these two variants of statism are we moving toward: socialism or fascism?"

"To answer this question," she said, "one must first ask: which is the dominant ideological trend of today's culture?

"The disgraceful and terrifying answer is: there is no ideological trend today. There is no ideology. There are no political principles, theories, ideals, or philosophy. There is no direction, no goal, no compass, no vision of the future, no intellectual element of leadership. Are there any emotional elements dominating today's culture? Yes! One! Fear!

"A country without a political philosophy is like a ship drifting at random in mid-ocean, at the mercy of any chance wind, wave, or current, a ship whose passengers huddle in their cabins and cry-- "Don't rock the boat!"—for fear of discovering that the captain's bridge is empty. (Bush is our captain)

"It is obvious that a boat which cannot stand rocking is doomed already and that it had better be rocked hard, if it is to regain its course—but this realization presupposes a grasp of facts, of reality, of principles and a long-range view, all of which are precisely the things that the "non-rockers" are frantically struggling to evade.

"Just as a neurotic believes that the facts of reality will vanish if he refuses to recognize them (Bush's current path)—so, today, the neurosis of an entire culture leads men to believe that their desperate need of political principles and concepts will vanish if they succeed in obliterating all principles and concepts. But since, in fact, neither an individual nor a nation can exist without some form of ideology, this sort of anti-ideology is now the formal, explicit, dominant ideology of our bankrupt culture. This anti-ideology has a new and very ugly name: it is called "Government by Consensus." Ayn Rand, Ford Hall Lecture, 1965

The noble citizen explained, "At some point in our history, we are going to have to deal with the "Mexicanization" of our Southwest and the

Left Coast. The issues are pretty simple, but they are too complicated for politicians because they involve money and intelligence.

"When mobs of illegals congregate in an American neighborhood, who is surprised that crime goes up? People who come illegally from Mexico often bring the "culture" of their home town with them, and that culture is the corrupt, immoral and scofflaw type that persists in Mexican cities. In Mexico, the cops are corrupt too, and whoever has the payola to keep them away--rules the neighborhood. The government is a bunch of "rich good old boys" in the Mexican sense, who aspire to greatness on top of a garbage heap. Only tourism and money sent home by illegals maintains stability.

"It is inevitable that politicians arising from this mass will manifest the culture from which they come. It's already happening, and the "what's in it for me" attitude of a lot of Hispanic politicians who cultivate the illegal "vote" and establishment of "citizen's rights" for illegals in places like southern California is subject to become epidemic in areas of high Mexican concentration. It's already costing the Southwestern states billions every year, just for infrastructure adjustment. So much for the "desirability" of having people who "do jobs Americans won't do." Americans are capable of mowing their own lawns and taking care of their own homes and children. This is a superfluous and specious argument, and does nothing to rationally support the millions of illegals establishing themselves every year on American territory.

"Yes, there are good people among them. But they are all illegals, and searching for a better life has different meanings depending on the level of cultural awareness and desire to assimilate. A separate Mexican community adds little to any city, and creates a lot of law enforcement problems. They bring corruption with them, and some of the problems are those of very dangerous and violent gang nature."

America's Ugly Ending

By Frosty Wooldridge

Reprinted by Permission

A listener on my radio show last week supported my guest's contention that California cannot be saved from its sinking into the morass of another Mexico City. Los Angeles Mayor Antonio Villiaragosa carries his La Raza and Mecha cards closer to his heart than the U.S. Constitution. Additionally he flies the Mexican flag in his office. Under his guidance, Mexico City's ugly reality created another horrible reality in Los Angeles.

The listener, Dean, said, "Your guest tonight covered a little of the news about how serious the illegal alien problem is in California. I lived in and around Los Angeles and Orange County areas for many years: 1943 to 1993. The dreadful destruction of the beautiful citrus groves and lush farm fields during the suffocating increase in population after WWII is not easy to describe in words that are graphic enough to convey the reality.

"A spokesman for the LAPD told National Public Radio recently that the LAPD had been overwhelmed by the rapidly growing street gangs. These gangs were, in years past, predominately the Negro outfits like the BLOODS and CRIPS. But, as the Mestizo illegals started coming in larger numbers, the Mestizo gangs muscled out the Negroes. Now, a new twist to the developing "civil war two" as predicted by Thomas Chittum in his book. The other ethnic factions are beginning to contend with the Mexican Mestizo gangs for control of the "turf" in Long Beach and the South Coast Los Angeles harbor districts.

"Samoans, Guamanians, Cambodians, Loatians, and Vietnamese gangs are asserting themselves. After the Rodney King riots in Los Angeles and Long Beach, the police have been forced to retreat into a defensive mode as the gangs gained more strength and territory. The violence has invaded formerly safe neighborhoods as law enforcement waned. I have long believed that the subversive outfits like La Raza have been involved in promoting the Mestizo outfits.

"The amount of spray paint used in their graffiti "tagging" activities is staggering. A four mile long section of the noise barrier walls built along the Long Beach Freeway near Firestone Blvd is covered with an incredible smear of gang designs and slogans spray painted over every square foot of the barrier walls which are approximately 10 feet in height. Overhead freeway direction signs over much of the Los Angeles freeway system are unreadable due to the multiple coats of graffiti on them.

"Before I left the area, the vandalism was spreading to the freeway signs in formerly "safe" Orange County. Unsolved hit-and-run shootings on the streets and freeways run into many, many cases. There were several cases occurring very near my place of employment near Wilmington and Supulveda Avenues in the Carson district. On the 4th of July and New Years eve, police vacate the streets and police helicopters don't fly. Why?

"Because of bullets from small arms fire! The LAPD will not serve a warrant in certain areas of Los Angeles without backup by a SWAT team. California is another IRAQ just waiting to happen as the ethnic factions become more aggressive. Thomas Chittum's book: "Civil War II: Coming Breakup of America" forecasts of a coming "civil war two" fueled by factions that have a mutual distrust and hatred for each other is not just a figment of the imagination. I hope that you can locate Thomas Chittum and get him to come on your radio program."

Just as I interviewed: <http://www.minutemanhq.com/>www.minutemanhq.com leader Chris Simcox last week, I will interview Thomas Chittum in the coming weeks. His book "In the 21st Century". I've read it. and it brought shudders up and down my spine. Why? Simple! You can see it happening all over the country.

To support the ugly mess in Los Angeles, another Mexican reader fits Chittum's profile of what we allowed into our country. This reader loves taunting me as I continue my weekly quixotic warnings concerning America's future. He signs off as Commandante Pedro.

"Surely you must realize all of your efforts, all of them, are futile? Your own government and elected representatives are aiding and abetting our Reconquista, and there is nothing you can do about it. Nothing! This is our country now. Can you honestly say California is an American state? Our people are firmly in charge there. Once the mid-term elections are over the government will move full speed ahead with a blanket amnesty and citizenship for all of the immigrants already here.

"This will cause a virtual flood of immigration as our brethren crash the gates and demand their human rights, citizenship, and social benefits. You, the white colonizer and pillager, will pay for it all! Once our brothers get the right to vote we will ensure that only those who agree with, or at least support our agenda stand for office. As the Borg would say, "resistance is futile." Death to the white man! Long live Aztlan! Long live the Bronze Age!

"Keep writing your useless warnings! I love reading your pathetic articles. Your attempts to galvanize the hoi polloi into action amuses me. Don't you realize that the average Joe six-pack white trash American doesn't give a s**t? He'll keep on swilling beer and watching Spike TV until the revolution begins in earnest and he is brought to account for the crimes of his forebears. Our allies in the media and academia have seen to it that the white man feels guilty and impotent in the face of his crimes. This is our country now; our women are lovely and pleasing to the eye, and the white man cannot get enough of them. We will defeat you by sheer force of numbers. All of your attempts are futile; your own politicians know that we are the future, that we must be taken into consideration whenever a major decision is made. The white vote means nothing. This is our time now. You had your time. The white man has been ascendant for centuries, now it is the time of the brown man. The best thing you can do for yourself is pack up and leave to northern Europe. You are no longer wanted. Does this make you angry? It is the truth nonetheless and you know it. Thanks be to God that you have been made a stranger in the land your ancestors stole! Viva Aztlan!"

Subcommandante Pedro MeCHA Brown Berets Infiltration Brigades Los Angeles, Baja California Aztlan

"P.S. I receive $721 social security monthly while working off the books, with complete medical insurance to boot. My wife receives welfare, food stamps, and childcare funds for our growing brood. Three of my children also receive generous social security checks. Only two of our six children are citizens. We are living very well and it is all thanks to the American taxpaying sucker. Muchas Gracias!"

The new amnesty bill by McCain-Kennedy legalizes 20 million illegal aliens with this kind of attitude while it allows chain migration and two million legal immigrants annually that will pack this country with 70 million immigrants from Mexico, Central and South America by 2040. If you think what you're seeing in Los Angeles disturbs you, wait until Chicago, New York City, Miami, Houston, San Francisco, Atlanta and other cities tip toward majority foreign trash populations. It's brought to you by President George Bush and Congress both Republican and Democrats. It will become increasingly ugly for Americans in America.

A week ago, hundreds of thousands of illegal aliens waving Mexican flags marched in America's streets, ironically, against our U.S. Constitution-and contrary to the rule of law. They possessed no right to be in our country and no rights while residing in our country. They demanded rights they had no right to demand.

"A man who thinks of himself as belonging to a particular national group in America has not yet become an American, and the man who goes among you to trade upon your nationality is not a worthy son to live under the Stars and Stripes." Woodrow Wilson, U.S. President

After breaking federal laws by barging into our country unlawfully, they demanded we change our laws to suit their purposes. They waved thousands of Mexican flags. When any army invades another country, it manifests dominance by raising its flag over the defeated nation. Think of our U.S. Marines planting Old Glory on Iwo Jima in WWII. Mexicana Airlines in their in-flight magazine, boasted, "With all due respect, Los Angeles is ours." Meanwhile, Mexicans succeeded in waving their flag on American soil in defiance of our sovereignty. They trampled the Stars and Stripes into the gutters of Los Angeles.

"We have room for but one flag, the American flag .....We have room for but one language here and that is the English language ....and we have room for but one sole loyalty, and that is a loyalty to the American people." Theodore Roosevelt

Against all common sense; against any kind of sanity; against the rule of law; against every lawful citizen and legal immigrant, our corrupt and cowardly U.S. Senate Judiciary Committee caved into 500,000 illegals' demands in Los Angeles and passed a bill that will give illegals amnesty for their crimes as well as a right to U.S. citizenship. How low can they degrade our citizenship in our own country? The sweep of this corruption of our Congress takes my breath way. Those guilty of treason are: Arlen Specter (R-PA) DeWine (R-OH) Graham (R-SC) Brownback (R-KS) Leahy (D-VT) Kennedy (D-MA) Biden (D-DE) Kohl (D-WI) Feinstein (D-CA) Feingold (D-WI) Schumer (D-NY) Durbin (D-IL)

Who are these miscreants that didn't stand up for our U.S. Constitution in the past 20 years in the first place? Who are these men selling out our country to this Mexican invasion? Who are these weasels in suits strutting around the halls of Congress, that if I met them face to face, I'd spit at their feet? They are fat, inane and useless old men hanging onto power even as they abdicate the reigns of law in their own country. These men represent foreign countries and corporations instead of American citizens.

The editors of Human Events ranked them as follows. These are the guys selling out to corporations and the U.S. Chamber of Commerce instead of standing up for American workers. They are a slimy bunch of politicians that would sell their country into civil war for a buck.

http://www.humaneventsonline.com/blog-detail.php?id=13565

From the least of them to the worst, here they are: meet them for what they are worth:

10. Senator Mike DeWine (R.-OH) Judiciary Committee member, voted for amnesty for agricultural workers, for spouses and children of illegals. He co-sponsored an in-state tuition bill for illegals. He opposed increasing funding for Border Patrol and adding more ICE agents. This man is a traitor to the people of Ohio. He needs to move to Mexico where he can represent Mexicans.

9. Senator Patrick Leahy (D.-VT) Ranking member of the Senate Judiciary Committee. He worked with Senator Specter on his amnesty-granting immigration bill. This man is incompetent and as useless as a senator representing Cuba. He stands for nothing the people of Vermont want-and that is, to stop illegal immigration.

8. Rep. Luis Gutierrez (D.-IL) He co-sponsored of the House version of McCain-Kennedy. This man, in sheep's clothing advocates for Mexicans and does everything he can to destroy our sovereignty as a country. He's like a scorpion that our country swallowed and now, he's stinging us from inside our belly.

7. Rep. Howard Berman (D.-CA) He accused Rep. James Sensenbrenner (R.-WI) of playing to the cheap seats with his bill to construct a border fence. He co-sponsored legislation to increase amnesties for spouses and children of illegals. This guy would have you pay for his children to go to your schools while he takes welfare checks that he never paid into. He's a traitor, plain and simple.

6. Rep. John Conyers (D.-MI) Co-sponsored legislation to grant amnesty to illegal aliens with a family member or employer willing to sponsor them. He will assume Judiciary

chairmanship if Democrats win control of the House in November. This guy is out to kill any understanding of what it means to be an American.

5. Rep. Nancy Pelosi (D.-CA) She consistently opposes any restrictions on immigration. She calls measures to criminalize illegal immigrants and those who assist them. She co-sponsored the SOLVE Act with Rep. Gutierrez to create a temporary guest-worker program. She is the handmaiden of opening our borders to an unending flood of immigrants. She would sell out her own family in a heart beat. She is selling out her own country before your eyes.

4. Senator Hillary Clinton (D.-NY) Once said she was adamantly against illegal immigrants. She now supports legalizing the 11 million illegals living in the U.S. She has vowed to block any bill criminalizing illegal immigration, suggested the House immigration bill would have made Jesus a criminal. As if she has stepped foot into a church in the last 40 years! Hillary Clinton is like a flag that flaps according to the direction of the wind.

3. Senator Arlen Specter (R.-PA) Judiciary Chairman, introduced a bill to convert illegal aliens into legal guest-workers for six years without first making them return to their home country and to allow more temporary workers and their families into the United States. He's old, intellectually inept and in control of our country's horrific destiny. This old man makes me sick as he attempts to double the current one million immigrants to two million annually. As if we don't already have our country filled with enough foreigners!

2. Senator Teddy Kennedy (D.-MA) He's the first O.J. Simpson! He's old, fat, drunk and has waddled around the halls of Congress for so long and blathered about nothing, that he's like antique plumbing: not working, stuffed up and useless. He's co-sponsoring legislation with McCain to grant amnesty to illegal aliens and has repeatedly supported amnesty efforts. He favors giving illegal students amnesty and a free college education. He's the author of the 1965

Immigration Reform Act that inundated this country with over 50 million immigrants that we didn't need in the first place. Now, he's overseen the addition of 20 million illegals that we don't want. He's going to force them down our throats anyway. That will pave the way for millions more.

1. Sen. John McCain (R.-AZ) He once served his country with honor, but today he leads with dishonor against our country. He's done nothing to stop the illegal invasion in his own state, but now, he's doing everything he can to assist illegal aliens across our country. He's the lead sponsor with Teddy Kennedy of a bill to grant amnesty to illegal aliens. He's degraded citizenship to the level of an illegal alien. He lacks honor and he lacks integrity for the U.S. Constitution.

Use this website to locate your Congressperson http://www.visi.com/ juan/congress/

US Congressional Switchboard Toll-free Numbers:

1-800-833-6354 ; 1-866-340-9281 ; 1-877-762-8762 ; 1-866-808-0065 ; 1-888-355-3588 ; 1-866-220-0044

Senators Brownback, Craig and Durbin snuck in the Dream Act into the Specter bill by giving illegal aliens in-state tuition at our expense while taking college slots from American kids, and the rest of the cowards in the U.S. Senate. Former Representative Duke Cunningham, now in prison for accepting $2.4 million in bribes from contractors, is the tip of the iceberg of corrupt congressmen destroying our Republic. They're spineless lapdogs for money and personal gain. My own Senator Wayne Allard (R-CO) featured a Mexican flag on his official senatorial website garnished with Spanish. Representative Chris Cannon of Utah along with Joe Baca of California do everything in their power to undermine our immigration laws. Their actions are the benchmark for treason against our Constitution. You can bet your senators and house representatives float in the same boat.

And who is the number one traitor? George W. Bush stands as the foremost traitor to his oath of office, his family and his country. He created the Iraq War with a lie and continues by lying to us. He accomplishes nothing except death and civil war for Iraq by keeping our troops in Iraq. His greatest transgression stands against the U.S. Constitution, which he reportedly has referred to as a "God damned piece of paper." A week ago, hundreds of thousands of illegal aliens waving Mexican flags marched in America's streets, ironically, against our U.S. Constitution-and contrary to the rule of law. They possessed no right to be in our country and no rights while residing in our country. They demanded rights they had no right to demand. What was done.? Nothing! Cowardly officials!

THE PLOT TO DESTROY AMERICA

TO BE OR NOT TO be, this is the question that Real Americans should be asking themselves. "Do I care enough for the future of America and my family to demand our president and politicians protect us or should I just let the traitors have their low down lying way and hope for the best even when I know it will result in destruction of America, or, should I as a loyal American prepare to defend my country against invading criminals to protect my family and property?

WITHIN THE ANSWER LIES THE fate of an America under fatal attack not only from our president and politicians but foreign criminal invaders suffocating and destroying America by sheer numbers. These invaders have no respect for America, no intention of becoming Americans and no intention of working to make America a better place to live and work – on the contrary. Trashing America just like the lousy Mexico they ran from to enter America illegally will be the total of their existence! Their announced purpose in life is to conquer America through the stupidity and apathy of Real American citizens asleep at the wheel. Their evil and dastardly plan is being promoted by our cowardly politicians who have no backbone and terminal Alzheimer's disease. Failure to defend America against this direct challenge to our constitution, our 230 year way of life, and a direct threat to kill gringos, is treason and betrayal to all American citizens. These elected officials including the president have sworn an oath when taking office to protect America against all enemies foreign and domestic….. so help me God! Are we being protected? The answer is obvious as The United States continues to be flooded by Illegal Immigrant Criminals, Crime gangs run rampant, police are ordered not to interfere with gang operations, and billions of TAXPAYER dollars are used to support freeloader criminals working to destroy our civilization! How does this rhyme with protecting America?

What aberration of a presumed once loyal American mind results in treachery and deceit? Is it an illusion of power, a lust for influence no one else has, a mindset of superior knowledge, just what is it that would lead a normal individual to betray the trust of fellow Americans and place his country into jeopardy including his own family's future? Some attribute it to losing touch with reality and facts of life, others declare it is just plain stupidity surfacing in response to perceived demands by lying "wolves in sheep" clothing among their flock! It has been stated with authority that during the tenure of George Bush as governor of Texas, over Ten Million Illegal Immigrants swarmed into America unhindered. Make no mistake – this man? Knew exactly what was going on – he planned it! Perhaps this fact alone will portray our president as he really is. Therefore, with this known fact as a reference, the weak minded among remaining politicians have assumed "if the president can do it so can we"

The only redeeming grace for this ultimate act of treachery against America and American citizens is Direct action to remove all Illegal Alien Criminals from the property of the United States of America! The cost is secondary! America for Americans. To hell with illegals! They are ILLEGAL – there is a universal law that criminal acts be punished. The penalty for being in America ILLEGALLY is deportation or prison camp! The American people will see to it that punishment is meted out to traitorous politicians.

Americans have choked on political treason long enough – now is the time to vomit it back in the face of the traitors!

If the reader has any further doubt that what you have read so far is not an accurate assessment of the imminent danger facing America, please examine the following descriptions of some of the criminal foreign organizations brazenly, and in the face of U.S.Law Enforcement, declaring the takeover of the United States of America.

WHAT IS AZTLAN?

The myth of Aztlan can best be explained by California's Santa Barbara School District's Chicano Studies textbook, "The Mexican American Heritage" by East Los Angeles high school teacher Carlos Jimenez. On page 84 there is a redrawn map of Mexico and the United States, showing Mexico with a full one-third more territory, all of it taken back from the United States. On page 107, it says "Latinos are now realizing that the power to control Aztlan may once again be in their hands."

Shown are the "repatriated" eight or nine states including Colorado, California, Arizona, Texas, Utah, New Mexico, Oregon and parts of Washington. According to the school text, Mexico is supposed to regain these territories as they rightly belong to the "mythical" homeland of Aztlan. On page 86, it says "...a free-trade agreement... promises...if Mexico is to allow the U.S. to invest in Mexico... then Mexico should...be allowed to freely export...Mexican labor. Obviously this would mean a re-evaluation of the border between the two countries as we know it today." Jimenez's Aztlan myth is further amplified at MEChA club meetings held at Santa Barbara Public Schools..

The book, paid for by American tax payers through rotten politics cites no references or footnotes, leaving school children totally dependent on their teacher to separate fact from opinion and political propaganda. The book teaches separatism, victimization, nationalism, completely lacks patriotism towards the United States, and promotes an open border policy. The book is 100 percent editorial -- the opinions of the author - scumbag!

WHAT IS RAZA

"LA RAZA" (THE RACE) IS a broad term which refers to those whose ancestry is indigenous to the area of Mexico (or "Aztlan"). MEChA members refer to themselves as "La Raza" or "Raza," but the term itself is used to indicate camaraderie among those in different organizations with the same objectives. There are a number of organizations who consider themselves to be La Raza.

The most visible of these groups are MEChA, The Brown Berets de Aztlan, OLA (Organization for the Liberation of Aztlan), La Raza Unida Party, and the "Nation of Aztlan" to name a few. Although the activism of these organizations vary from somewhat radical to extremely radical, they share the same objectives, the "liberation of Aztlan." Each follows the Raza manifesto "El Plan de Aztlan (sometimes called "El Plan Espiritual de Aztlan"). The Nation of Aztlan, tied to La Voz de Aztlan disseminates the exact same propaganda that MEChA spreads including antisemitic propaganda. Believers in the Aztlan legend insist upon the indivisibility of "La Raza" and their common goals, one of them being the need to abolish the border between the U.S. and Mexico. There is a myriad of Raza college newspaper. Some are El Popo, Aztlan News, Chispas, Gente de Aztlan (UCLA), Voz Fronteriza (U.C. San Diego), La Voz Mestiza (U.C. Irvine) and La Voz Berkeley. It is not uncommon for the writers of these publications to refer to the U.S., as "AmeriKKKa."

Rhetoric by some Chicano educators strongly suggest Communist or Socialist leanings. In May, 2000, more than 1,200 students gathered at UCLA for the seventh annual Raza Youth Conference, which the members say promotes higher education and recognition of the Aztlan culture. Sponsored by MEChA, the year's theme was "Reclaiming Our Razas through education, resistance, and promoting the idea of remembering the historical struggles of Raza" said Erika Ramirez, co-chair of the conference. The conference drew students from 80 middle and high schools and community colleges; featured speeches by those actively involved with the Chicano community.

The keynote speaker was Antonia Darder, a professor of education and cultural studies at Claremont Graduate University and director of the Institute for Cultural Studies in Education, who received a standing ovation for her speech.

Darder described American capitalism and what she said were its impacts on racism and sexism. "I grew up in a capitalist society, a society that taught us that the greed of corporations control politics," Darder said. "Capitalism is the root of domination. Racism and sexism exist because capitalism requires it." Darder said a globalized economy forced smaller countries to give up their self-sufficiency, resulting in people migrating to the U.S. "We're here because U.S. foreign policy in Latin America has forced us here," she said.

The University of Oregon Chapter of MEChA hints at its communist sentiments by posting a picture of Cuba's communist dictator Fidel Castro. On its web site, "La Voz de Aztlan" has an excerpt from a speech of February 7, 1997, by Fidel Castro who said "the United States should return to Mexico huge chunks of that country's territories it acquired more than a century ago" La Voz de Aztlan, whom Antonio Villaraigosa refuses to repudiate, also disseminates antisemitic propaganda,

Apparently, these "Raza" cults are composed of people who unabashedly hate the United States and often support other groups and leaders who also hate America. Raza's hatred of America is so intense, that most make bedfellows to anyone else who also hates America, like dictator Fidel Castro; murderer of his own people Sadam Hussain; and the women hating Taliban -- and of course they sympathize with all Islamic Terrorists over the Israel/Palestine issue. Raza cults are the loudest and most insistent element of the immigration lobby in California. Inebriated with a sense of righteous victimhood, and entranced by myths (lies) of a heroic racial past, devotees of the Aztlan cults are rapidly extending their influence within California's Hispanic population, particularly among students in the university system. (Typical ignorance).

What is MEChA?

The acronym MEChA stands for "Movimiento Estudiantil Chicano de Aztlan." or "Chicano Student Movement of Aztlan."

MEChA is an Hispanic separatist organization that encourages anti-American activities and civil disobedience. The radical members of MEChA who refer to themselves as "Mechistas," romanticize Mexican claims to the "lost Territories" of the Southwestern United States -- a Chicano country called Aztlan. In its national constitution, MEChA calls for self-determination by its members to liberate Aztlan. MEChA's national constitution starts out: "Chicano and Chicana students of Aztlán must take upon themselves the responsibilities to promote Chicanismo within the community, politicizing our Raza with an emphasis on indigenous consciousness to continue the struggle for the self-determination of the Chicano people for the purpose of liberating Aztlán."

These anti-American "Mechistas" live with the false illusion that they are being racially discriminated against because they are Latinos while totally dismissing the idea that maybe it is their ideology that is being discriminated against.

At the MEChA National Conference on March 15 - 18, 2001, the official "MEChA Philosophy" was ratified. An excerpt from the document states: "as Mechistas, we vow to work for the liberation of Aztlan."

The MEChA Clubs on each of the Santa Barbara high school campuses are not the only ones. MEChA groups exist on 90 percent of the public high school, college and university campuses in the Southwestern United States.

Below are the names, addresses in Washington, and telephone numbers of our group of 100 so-called United States Senators duly elected by the people and for the people. Now, they are confronted with the inescapable destruction of America by Illegal Criminals and most of them have lost their nerve to stand up like Real Americans and do whatever is necessary to remove the hordes of invaders. Select your Senators and inform them in no uncertain terms that they will be ousted from office if they refuse to stand up for the rights of REAL Americans!

It's time to get America back on the path to Government of the people, by the people, and for the people, as so eloquently spoken by Abraham Lincoln.

> To contact Senators by eMail, place cursor on web form address next to desired name, hold down Ctrl key and click mouse. Write, call or eMail your Senators in the above lists and give them your opinion of their actions against America – in no uncertain terms – and do it now if you love your country – 62 of them don't!

UNITED STATES SENATORS

Senators of the 110th Congress
Sort by: Name   State   Party

| Choose a State ▾ | Choose a Senator ▾ | Choose a Class ▾ |

What is a class?

Akaka, Daniel K.- (D - HI)
141 HART SENATE OFFICE BUILDING WASHINGTON DC 20510
(202) 224-6361
Web Form: akaka.senate.gov/email.cfm

Alexander, Lamar- (R - TN)
455 DIRKSEN SENATE OFFICE BUILDING WASHINGTON DC 20510
(202) 224-4944
Web Form: alexander.senate.gov/index.cfm?FuseAction=Contact.Home

Allard, Wayne- (R - CO)
521 DIRKSEN SENATE OFFICE BUILDING WASHINGTON DC 20510
(202) 224-5941
Web Form: allard.senate.gov/public/index.cfm?FuseAction=Contact.Home

Baucus, Max- (D - MT)
511 HART SENATE OFFICE BUILDING WASHINGTON DC 20510
(202) 224-2651
Web Form: baucus.senate.gov/contact/emailForm.cfm?subj=issue

Bayh, Evan- (D - IN)
131 RUSSELL SENATE OFFICE BUILDING WASHINGTON DC 20510
(202) 224-5623
Web Form: bayh.senate.gov/WebMail1.htm

Bennett, Robert F.- (R - UT)
431 DIRKSEN SENATE OFFICE BUILDING WASHINGTON DC 20510
(202) 224-5444
Web Form: bennett.senate.gov/contact/emailmain.html

Biden, Joseph R., Jr.- (D - DE)
201 RUSSELL SENATE OFFICE BUILDING WASHINGTON DC 20510
(202) 224-5042
Web Form: biden.senate.gov/contact/emailjoe.cfm

Bingaman, Jeff- (D - NM)
703 HART SENATE OFFICE BUILDING WASHINGTON DC 20510
(202) 224-5521
E-mail: senator_bingaman@bingaman.senate.gov

Bond, Christopher S.- (R - MO)
274 RUSSELL SENATE OFFICE BUILDING WASHINGTON DC 20510
(202) 224-5721
Web Form: bond.senate.gov/contact/contactme.cfm

Boxer, Barbara- (D - CA)
112 HART SENATE OFFICE BUILDING WASHINGTON DC 20510
(202) 224-3553
Web Form: boxer.senate.gov/contact

Brown, Sherrod- (D - OH)
455 RUSSELL SENATE OFFICE BUILDING WASHINGTON DC 20510
(202) 224-2315
Web Form: brown.senate.gov/contact.cfm

Brownback, Sam- (R - KS)
303 HART SENATE OFFICE BUILDING WASHINGTON DC 20510
(202) 224-6521
Web Form: brownback.senate.gov/CMEmailMe.cfm

Bunning, Jim- (R - KY)
316 HART SENATE OFFICE BUILDING WASHINGTON DC 20510
(202) 224-4343
Web Form: bunning.senate.gov/index.cfm?FuseAction=Contact.Email

Burr, Richard- (R - NC)
217 RUSSELL SENATE OFFICE BUILDING WASHINGTON DC 20510
(202) 224-3154
Web Form: burr.senate.gov/index.cfm?FuseAction=Contact.Home

Byrd, Robert C.- (D - WV)
311 HART SENATE OFFICE BUILDING WASHINGTON DC 20510
(202) 224-3954
Web Form: byrd.senate.gov/byrd_email.html

Cantwell, Maria- (D - WA)
511 DIRKSEN SENATE OFFICE BUILDING WASHINGTON DC 20510
(202) 224-3441
Web Form: cantwell.senate.gov/contact/index.html

Cardin, Benjamin L.- (D - MD)
509 HART SENATE OFFICE BUILDING WASHINGTON DC 20510
(202) 224-4524
Web Form: cardin.senate.gov/contact/

Carper, Thomas R.- (D - DE)
513 HART SENATE OFFICE BUILDING WASHINGTON DC 20510
(202) 224-2441
Web Form: carper.senate.gov/aemail.htm

Casey, Robert P., Jr.- (D - PA)
383 RUSSELL SENATE OFFICE BUILDING WASHINGTON DC 20510
(202) 224-6324
Web Form: casey.senate.gov/contact.cfm

Chambliss, Saxby- (R - GA)
416 RUSSELL SENATE OFFICE BUILDING WASHINGTON DC 20510
(202) 224-3521
Web Form: chambliss.senate.gov/public/index.cfm?FuseAction=ContactU...

Clinton, Hillary Rodham- (D - NY)
476 RUSSELL SENATE OFFICE BUILDING WASHINGTON DC 20510
(202) 224-4451
Web Form: clinton.senate.gov/contact

Coburn, Tom- (R - OK)
172 RUSSELL SENATE OFFICE BUILDING WASHINGTON DC 20510
(202) 224-5754
Web Form: coburn.senate.gov/index.cfm?FuseAction=Contact.Home

Cochran, Thad- (R - MS)
113 DIRKSEN SENATE OFFICE BUILDING WASHINGTON DC 20510
(202) 224-5054
Web Form: cochran.senate.gov/contact.htm

Coleman, Norm- (R - MN)
320 HART SENATE OFFICE BUILDING WASHINGTON DC 20510
(202) 224-5641
Web Form: coleman.senate.gov/index.cfm?FuseAction=Contact.ContactForm

Collins, Susan M.- (R - ME)
413 DIRKSEN SENATE OFFICE BUILDING WASHINGTON DC 20510
(202) 224-2523
Web Form: collins.senate.gov/public/continue.cfm?FuseAction=Contact...

Conrad, Kent- (D - ND)
530 HART SENATE OFFICE BUILDING WASHINGTON DC 20510
(202) 224-2043
Web Form: conrad.senate.gov/webform.html

Corker, Bob- (R - TN)
185 DIRKSEN SENATE OFFICE BUILDING WASHINGTON DC 20510

(202) 224-3344
Web Form: corker.senate.gov/Contact/index.cfm

Cornyn, John- (R - TX)
517 HART SENATE OFFICE BUILDING WASHINGTON DC 20510
(202) 224-2934
Web Form: cornyn.senate.gov/contact/index.html

Craig, Larry E.- (R - ID)
520 HART SENATE OFFICE BUILDING WASHINGTON DC 20510
(202) 224-2752
Web Form: craig.senate.gov/email/

Crapo, Mike- (R - ID)
239 DIRKSEN SENATE OFFICE BUILDING WASHINGTON DC 20510
(202) 224-6142
Web Form: crapo.senate.gov/contact/email.cfm

DeMint, Jim- (R - SC)
340 RUSSELL SENATE OFFICE BUILDING WASHINGTON DC 20510
(202) 224-6121
Web Form: demint.senate.gov/index.cfm?FuseAction=Contact.Home

Dodd, Christopher J.- (D - CT)
448 RUSSELL SENATE OFFICE BUILDING WASHINGTON DC 20510
(202) 224-2823
Web Form: dodd.senate.gov/index.php?q=node/3130

Dole, Elizabeth- (R - NC)
555 DIRKSEN SENATE OFFICE BUILDING WASHINGTON DC 20510
(202) 224-6342
Web Form: dole.senate.gov/index.cfm?FuseAction=ContactInformation.C...

Domenici, Pete V.- (R - NM)
328 HART SENATE OFFICE BUILDING WASHINGTON DC 20510
(202) 224-6621
Web Form: domenici.senate.gov/contact/contactform.cfm

Dorgan, Byron L.- (D - ND)
322 HART SENATE OFFICE BUILDING WASHINGTON DC 20510
(202) 224-2551
E-mail: senator@dorgan.senate.gov

Durbin, Richard- (D - IL)
309 HART SENATE OFFICE BUILDING WASHINGTON DC 20510
(202) 224-2152
Web Form: durbin.senate.gov/contact.cfm

Ensign, John- (R - NV)
119 RUSSELL SENATE OFFICE BUILDING WASHINGTON DC 20510
(202) 224-6244
Web Form: ensign.senate.gov/forms/email_form.cfm

Enzi, Michael B.- (R - WY)
379A RUSSELL SENATE OFFICE BUILDING WASHINGTON DC 20510
(202) 224-3424
Web Form: enzi.senate.gov/public/index.cfm?FuseAction=ContactInform...

Feingold, Russell D.- (D - WI)
506 HART SENATE OFFICE BUILDING WASHINGTON DC 20510
(202) 224-5323
Web Form: feingold.senate.gov/contact_opinion.html

Feinstein, Dianne- (D - CA)
331 HART SENATE OFFICE BUILDING WASHINGTON DC 20510
(202) 224-3841
Web Form: feinstein.senate.gov/email.html

Graham, Lindsey- (R - SC)
290 RUSSELL SENATE OFFICE BUILDING WASHINGTON DC 20510
(202) 224-5972
Web Form: lgraham.senate.gov/index.cfm?mode=contact

Grassley, Chuck- (R - IA)
135 HART SENATE OFFICE BUILDING WASHINGTON DC 20510
(202) 224-3744
Web Form: grassley.senate.gov/index.cfm?FuseAction=Contact.Home

Gregg, Judd- (R - NH)
393 RUSSELL SENATE OFFICE BUILDING WASHINGTON DC 20510
(202) 224-3324
Web Form: gregg.senate.gov/sitepages/contact.cfm

Hagel, Chuck- (R - NE)
248 RUSSELL SENATE OFFICE BUILDING WASHINGTON DC 20510
(202) 224-4224
Web Form: hagel.senate.gov/index.cfm?FuseAction=Contact.Home

Harkin, Tom- (D - IA)
731 HART SENATE OFFICE BUILDING WASHINGTON DC 20510
(202) 224-3254
Web Form: harkin.senate.gov/contact/contact.cfm

Hatch, Orrin G.- (R - UT)
104 HART SENATE OFFICE BUILDING WASHINGTON DC 20510
(202) 224-5251
Web Form: hatch.senate.gov/index.cfm?Fuseaction=Offices.Contact

Hutchison, Kay Bailey- (R - TX)
284 RUSSELL SENATE OFFICE BUILDING WASHINGTON DC 20510
(202) 224-5922
Web Form: hutchison.senate.gov/contact.html

Inhofe, James M.- (R - OK)
453 RUSSELL SENATE OFFICE BUILDING WASHINGTON DC 20510
(202) 224-4721
Web Form: inhofe.senate.gov/contactus.htm

Inouye, Daniel K.- (D - HI)
722 HART SENATE OFFICE BUILDING WASHINGTON DC 20510
(202) 224-3934
Web Form: inouye.senate.gov/abtform.html

Isakson, Johnny- (R - GA)
120 RUSSELL SENATE OFFICE BUILDING WASHINGTON DC 20510
(202) 224-3643
Web Form: isakson.senate.gov/contact.cfm

Johnson, Tim- (D - SD)
136 HART SENATE OFFICE BUILDING WASHINGTON DC 20510
(202) 224-5842
Web Form: johnson.senate.gov/emailform.cfm

Kennedy, Edward M.- (D - MA)
317 RUSSELL SENATE OFFICE BUILDING WASHINGTON DC 20510
(202) 224-4543
Web Form: kennedy.senate.gov/senator/contact.cfm

Kerry, John F.- (D - MA)
304 RUSSELL SENATE OFFICE BUILDING WASHINGTON DC 20510
(202) 224-2742
Web Form: kerry.senate.gov/v3/contact/email.html

Klobuchar, Amy- (D - MN)
302 HART SENATE OFFICE BUILDING WASHINGTON DC 20510
(202) 224-3244
Web Form: klobuchar.senate.gov/contact.cfm

Kohl, Herb- (D - WI)
330 HART SENATE OFFICE BUILDING WASHINGTON DC 20510

(202) 224-5653
Web Form: kohl.senate.gov/gen_contact.html

Kyl, Jon- (R - AZ)
730 HART SENATE OFFICE BUILDING WASHINGTON DC 20510
(202) 224-4521
Web Form: kyl.senate.gov/contact.cfm

Landrieu, Mary L.- (D - LA)
724 HART SENATE OFFICE BUILDING WASHINGTON DC 20510
(202) 224-5824
Web Form: landrieu.senate.gov/contact/index.cfm

Lautenberg, Frank R.- (D - NJ)
324 HART SENATE OFFICE BUILDING WASHINGTON DC 20510
(202) 224-3224
Web Form: lautenberg.senate.gov/contact/

Leahy, Patrick J.- (D - VT)
433 RUSSELL SENATE OFFICE BUILDING WASHINGTON DC 20510
(202) 224-4242
E-mail: senator_leahy@leahy.senate.gov

Levin, Carl- (D - MI)
269 RUSSELL SENATE OFFICE BUILDING WASHINGTON DC 20510
(202) 224-6221
Web Form: levin.senate.gov/contact/index.cfm

Lieberman, Joseph I.- (ID - CT)
706 HART SENATE OFFICE BUILDING WASHINGTON DC 20510
(202) 224-4041
Web Form: lieberman.senate.gov/contact/index.cfm?regarding=issue

---

Lincoln, Blanche L.- (D - AR)
355 DIRKSEN SENATE OFFICE BUILDING WASHINGTON DC 20510
(202) 224-4843
Web Form: lincoln.senate.gov/webform.html

Lott, Trent- (R - MS)
487 RUSSELL SENATE OFFICE BUILDING WASHINGTON DC 20510
(202) 224-6253
Web Form: lott.senate.gov/index.cfm?FuseAction=Contact.Email

Lugar, Richard G.- (R - IN)
306 HART SENATE OFFICE BUILDING WASHINGTON DC 20510
(202) 224-4814
E-mail: senator_lugar@lugar.senate.gov

Martinez, Mel- (R - FL)
356 RUSSELL SENATE OFFICE BUILDING WASHINGTON DC 20510
(202) 224-3041
Web Form: martinez.senate.gov/public/index.cfm?FuseAction=ContactIn...

McCain, John- (R - AZ)
241 RUSSELL SENATE OFFICE BUILDING WASHINGTON DC 20510
(202) 224-2235
Web Form: mccain.senate.gov/index.cfm?fuseaction=Contact.Home

McCaskill, Claire- (D - MO)
717 HART SENATE OFFICE BUILDING WASHINGTON DC 20510
(202) 224-6154
Web Form: mccaskill.senate.gov/contact.cfm

McConnell, Mitch- (R - KY)
361-A RUSSELL SENATE OFFICE BUILDING WASHINGTON DC 20510
(202) 224-2541
Web Form: mcconnell.senate.gov/contact_form.cfm

Menendez, Robert- (D - NJ)
317 HART SENATE OFFICE BUILDING WASHINGTON DC 20510
(202) 224-4744
Web Form: menendez.senate.gov/contact/contact.cfm

Mikulski, Barbara A.- (D - MD)
503 HART SENATE OFFICE BUILDING WASHINGTON DC 20510
(202) 224-4654
Web Form: mikulski.senate.gov/mailform.html

Murkowski, Lisa- (R - AK)
709 HART SENATE OFFICE BUILDING WASHINGTON DC 20510
(202) 224-6665
Web Form: murkowski.senate.gov/contact.cfm

Murray, Patty- (D - WA)
173 RUSSELL SENATE OFFICE BUILDING WASHINGTON DC 20510
(202) 224-2621
Web Form: murray.senate.gov/email/index.cfm

Nelson, Bill- (D - FL)
716 HART SENATE OFFICE BUILDING WASHINGTON DC 20510
(202) 224-5274
Web Form: billnelson.senate.gov/contact/email.cfm

Nelson, E. Benjamin- (D - NE)
720 HART SENATE OFFICE BUILDING WASHINGTON DC 20510
(202) 224-6551
Web Form: bennelson.senate.gov/contact/email.cfm

Obama, Barack- (D - IL)
713 HART SENATE OFFICE BUILDING WASHINGTON DC 20510
(202) 224-2854
Web Form: obama.senate.gov/contact/

Pryor, Mark L.- (D - AR)
257 DIRKSEN SENATE OFFICE BUILDING WASHINGTON DC 20510
(202) 224-2353
Web Form: pryor.senate.gov/contact/

Reed, Jack- (D - RI)
728 HART SENATE OFFICE BUILDING WASHINGTON DC 20510
(202) 224-4642
Web Form: reed.senate.gov/contact/contact-share.cfm

Reid, Harry- (D - NV)
528 HART SENATE OFFICE BUILDING WASHINGTON DC 20510
(202) 224-3542
Web Form: reid.senate.gov/contact/email_form.cfm

Roberts, Pat- (R - KS)
109 HART SENATE OFFICE BUILDING WASHINGTON DC 20510
(202) 224-4774
Web Form: roberts.senate.gov/public/index.cfm?FuseAction=ContactInf...

Rockefeller, John D., IV- (D - WV)
531 HART SENATE OFFICE BUILDING WASHINGTON DC 20510
(202) 224-6472
Web Form: rockefeller.senate.gov/services/email.cfm

Salazar, Ken- (D - CO)
702 HART SENATE OFFICE BUILDING WASHINGTON DC 20510
(202) 224-5852
Web Form: salazar.senate.gov/contact/email.cfm

Sanders, Bernard- (I - VT)
332 DIRKSEN SENATE OFFICE BUILDING WASHINGTON DC 20510
(202) 224-5141
Web Form: sanders.senate.gov/comments/

Schumer, Charles E.- (D - NY)
313 HART SENATE OFFICE BUILDING WASHINGTON DC 20510

(202) 224-6542
Web Form: schumer.senate.gov/SchumerWebsite/contact/webform.cfm

Sessions, Jeff- (R - AL)
335 RUSSELL SENATE OFFICE BUILDING WASHINGTON DC 20510
(202) 224-4124
Web Form: sessions.senate.gov/email/contact.cfm

Shelby, Richard C.- (R - AL)
110 HART SENATE OFFICE BUILDING WASHINGTON DC 20510
(202) 224-5744
E-mail: senator@shelby.senate.gov

Smith, Gordon H.- (R - OR)
404 RUSSELL SENATE OFFICE BUILDING WASHINGTON DC 20510
(202) 224-3753
Web Form: gsmith.senate.gov/webform.htm

Snowe, Olympia J.- (R - ME)
154 RUSSELL SENATE OFFICE BUILDING WASHINGTON DC 20510
(202) 224-5344
Web Form: snowe.senate.gov/contact.htm

Specter, Arlen- (R - PA)
711 HART SENATE OFFICE BUILDING WASHINGTON DC 20510
(202) 224-4254
Web Form: specter.senate.gov/index.cfm?FuseAction=ContactInfo.Home

Stabenow, Debbie- (D - MI)
133 HART SENATE OFFICE BUILDING WASHINGTON DC 20510
(202) 224-4822
Web Form: stabenow.senate.gov/email.htm

Stevens, Ted- (R - AK)
522 HART SENATE OFFICE BUILDING WASHINGTON DC 20510
(202) 224-3004
Web Form: stevens.senate.gov/public/index.cfm?FuseAction=Contact.Em...

Sununu, John E.- (R - NH)
111 RUSSELL SENATE OFFICE BUILDING WASHINGTON DC 20510
(202) 224-2841
Web Form: www.sununu.senate.gov/webform.html

Tester, Jon- (D - MT)
204 RUSSELL SENATE OFFICE BUILDING WASHINGTON DC 20510
(202) 224-2644
Web Form: tester.senate.gov/Contact/

In Conclusion :
The Final Frontier

AMERICA HAS WEATHERED MANY ATTACKS on an unheard concept of human existence and endeavor and at the expense of the lives and crippling injuries of hundreds of thousands of brave men and women, and has survived and continued to offer freedoms and opportunities non-existent anywhere else.

Now however, America is facing her greatest threat in 230 years of world envy. As our forefathers warned, people chosen to carry on the nation's business as representatives of citizens, must be watched closely. This caution has proved to be 100% correct! For the past 50 years, a majority of those we elected and trusted have betrayed the people through deceit, lying, stealing and personal agendas. The many opportunities available to profit handsomely from only one elected term has enticed many to make felonious promises to big business entities in order to get elected. There can be only one outcome of paid-for loyalty – treasonous disservice to American citizens and America! Incompetence and arrogance soon follows and loyalty to the people and America becomes a thing of the past. Personal gratification then becomes the primary purpose of the trusted position and sincere concerns for the national welfare is subservient to personal profiteering. America is and has been betrayed by the incestuous greed of "big business" ambitions for many years; it makes no difference which political party is in power at the moment. The treason continues unabated! The stupid rotten politicians and big business racketeers will be the first to be killed by the invading hordes - hoisted on their own petard of greed and treason to America.

Common sense is booted off the throne of reasoning and in it's place sex and immorality are hailed as king. People of low moral character and high mental susceptibility are impressed by rotten government "power individuals", mistakenly believing in their integrity and loyalty. Little does the average dumb uninformed American who has placed unwarranted trust in elected officials realize the extent of graft, deceit, lying and total disregard for the safety and welfare of our nation that exists throughout our government political leaders. Our own President George Bush (Poor Little Rich Boy), has forsaken Real Americans and welcomes millions of Illegal Criminals to America while ignoring the subversive activities of Mexican officials and outright calls to kill Gringos. The stinking and rotten acts of treason by traitorous political leaders from top to bottom is pointing out with glaring confirmation the warnings of our nation's founders: Contamination of citizen ethics soon becomes a national epidemic of imitating the traitors as "Let The Good Times Roll" becomes the national pastime! Total inattention by elected politicians and citizens as to the swelling infiltration of society by those eager to occupy and claim America as their home! Suddenly, it becomes apparent that Illegal Immigrants from Mexico have reached prodigious populations thru the totally reckless birthrate coupled with ignorance and disregard as to what they are doing. Now we have a situation unforeseen, which could have been prevented by positive and purposeful action, developing into demands for considerations and services normally reserved for American citizens only. The cost to satisfy these demands amount to billions that should be allocated to the infrastructure repair. However, cowardice is resorted to in order to prevent demonstrations in the streets by illegal criminals and money is provided for illegal child birth, schools, clothing, transportation and medical treatment. Consternation sets in and hand wringing accompanied by guilt through desertion of patriotism due to cowardice having the upper hand. The Illegal Criminals sensing this as an indication of weakness – (Is this surprising) ? Begins to organize arrogant demonstrations demanding their rights to be accepted as citizens of a country they invaded. Next, thoughts of appeasement begin to develop in some of the old sick minds as a means to smooth things over and perhaps the situation will be solved by offering some version of amnesty. Never mind that America will be trashed and trampled into the dirt by these ignorant and mindless hordes intent on destroying the Gringos.

It has become painfully obvious from a historical review of American society in the last fifty years, that forces of evil and deceit from politicians, shadowy bastions of once prized learning institutions, so-called civil rights organizations, self gratification, favoritism and corruption have superseded loyalty and patriotism to America! Today's America is in shambles, a shameful and disgraceful comparison to the great nation of yesterday! Corporate corruption scandals, improper (crooked) behavior of political figures, sex scandals, and total abandonment of sworn oaths of office of some of our top political figures have become commonplace. If this is the attitude and performance of these officials, corporate and governmental, then what can be the inevitable result but that this is interpreted by a huge percentage of morally corruptible American citizens as being officially sanctioned? As time progresses and more and more instances of malfeasance are publicized, decadent behavior patterns emulating many of the miserable and disgusting trusted officials begin to emerge and accepted as "normal". This, then, is transformed into an attitude and motivation of "Let The Good Times Roll" that includes wide open sexual behavior, increasing use and reliance on drugs, murder, rape, sodomy, robbery for drugs and family destruction! In addition, a secondary massive destructive effect is passed on to include school children encouraged to try drugs. Now we have a pattern of lives destroyed by drugs, immorality, murder by school children, and no concern for the nation for which millions of Americans have made the ultimate sacrifice to protect future generations! There can be but one eventual result of this tragic and suicidal situation. Death of America! When a nation's leaders, corporate and political, Presidential and Vice-Presidential, trusted and relied upon, betray and fail their sworn oaths and responsibilities, there can be no other result! Can this path to destruction and oblivion be cut off and directed toward salvation of America? The answer lies with throwing out our rotten Political leadership by whatever option is necessary! America's elected representatives must stand up and present and obligate themselves in an honest dedicated purpose for America. To respond to outside influences and criticisms with apologies is a betrayal of their sworn oath and only results in increased boldness and aggressiveness of foreign idiots who will trash America. In addition they must offer real relief to millions of downtrodden forgotten Americans who have been abandoned! Severe punishment must be meted out to those corporate crooks who steal millions from their companies and deprive employees of a decent future. Political dishonesty must be internally policed by members and associates with public disclosure of criminal and immoral acts plus impeachment and disgrace! The American people must wake up, come to attention and pass sentence on the fitness of those chosen to lead America in our place.

Not only the perceived morality of our government but also performance reality must be one of dedication and honesty, based on the beliefs of the founders of America which has been proved for 230 years but is now in the process of being abdicated by Politically Correct politicians. Our soldiers believe in America, why not those we have elected to stand in our place?

Again : There is no nation on earth more corrupt than the United States of America. Corruption in America is like an iceberg, which has one tenth exposed and nine tenths hidden.

The present Collapse of America rests on the shoulders of George Bush and the traitors in the Senate and House of Representatives – most are too sick and old to serve with the energy of a clean mind and body.

America is in desperate need of many more dedicated men like Representative Tom Tancredo, Representative Dana Rahrabacher, and Representative Duncan Hunter.

Take a moment and reflect on the following:

James Madison our fourth President said:

"Although men are born free, slavery has been the general lot of the human race. When ignorant they have been cheated, when asleep they have been surprised and divided, and the yoke of tyranny forced upon them. But what is the lesson ?....the people should stay enlightened, to be awake, to be united and watch over a government… it has been demonstrated that only a well instructed people can be permanently free."

President Theodore Roosevelt said :

" Behind the ostensible government sits enthroned an invisible government owing no allegiance and acknowledging no responsibility to the people."

He was correct: CFL, NAU, World Order, One World Treason.

"It is only when the people become ignorant and corrupt, when they degenerate into a populace, that they are incapable of exercising their sovereignty. Usurpation is then an easy attainment, and a usurper soon found. The people themselves become the willing instruments of their own debasement and ruin." Author Unknown.

Thomas Jefferson said:

"… if the people do not keep the government as a slave, they themselves shall wind up as slaves!"

Thomas Jefferson said:

"Experience hath shewn, that even under the best forms of government those entrusted with power have, in time and by slow operations, perverted it into tyranny!"

Thomas Jefferson said in 1787:

"Lethargy is the forerunner of death to the public liberty."

"For those who guide this people are leading them astray…. and those who are guided by them are brought to confusion… and by their smooth flattering speech they deceive the hearts of the unsuspecting" (Isaiah 9:16, Romans 16:18)

History should have taught us : Men of Power need to be watched!

Wake Up Real Americans –America is   being betrayed by those we trust!

Support Impeachments

www.ingramcontent.com/pod-product-compliance
Lightning Source LLC
Chambersburg PA
CBHW031321290526
45784CB00014B/606